FINGER GRIPS
ETCHED IN FAITH

FINGER GRIPS ETCHED IN FAITH

STAYING
THE
COURSE OF LIFE

ANDREW FRIERSON, JR

Order this book online at www.trafford.com
or email orders@trafford.com

Most Trafford titles are also available at major online book retailers.

Printed in the United States of America.

ISBN: 978-1-4269-6343-8 (sc)
ISBN: 978-1-4269-6344-5 (hc)
ISBN: 978-1-4269-6345-2 (e)

Library of Congress Control Number: 2011904840

Trafford rev. 05/06/2011

 www.trafford.com

North America & international
toll-free: 1 888 232 4444 (USA & Canada)
phone: 250 383 6864 ♦ fax: 812 355 4082

To my parents, Andrew and Althea, both committed their love and devotion, to pouring themselves into the lives of their children.

PREFACE

Finger Grips Etched in Faith, is my sharing a lifetime of compelling experiences. Calling upon my memory, it releases those experiences in frames and periods of time. Each one, revealing wise lessons, and instructive insights, that for me, in youth, held little value. As my age and maturity advanced, those lessons and insights have vividly resurfaced. They are still, potent jewels of wisdom, and vignettes of instruction. I wonder why I rejected them earlier when I could have benefited from their guidance. The answer is that youth, too often, thrives on denial and ignorance; both tend to overrule good judgment.

The wisdom life offers does not wait around when not utilized. However, it reserves itself to be given out by the very ones who rejected it earlier. Having missed the benefit the first time, the value becomes to them as gold. So, I share today, my golden nuggets of wisdom, gleaned from yesterday's indifference. May their brightness help light the way for generational travelers?

Another motivation for writing this book is to empower my family in their knowledge of our heritage. I believe "Finger Grips Etched in Faith" will provide a foundation succeeding family generations can build on. My story will automatically dovetail into some of the events I and my nine siblings shared. While each sibling's memories are determined by their own personal experiences; I hope mine; given from my personal journey, will help the family story evolve to full perspective. Each time we meet, we unconsciously edit our history through our sharing. As this is done, our individual contributions, closes any gaps of knowledge, or intimacy between sibling age differences. This is important, because of the fifteen year span between the first and the last child of Andrew, and Althea.

When the filling in, and the sharing of stories, of the ten siblings is complete; there will be one picture, from ten perspectives. As succeeding generations evolve, I hope each will close ranks, and keep the family strong. This will require real effort to keep the gaps between generations at a minimum. New technologies, geological changes and time itself work against family intimacy. This new age of social net working, if utilized can be a valuable asset to maintaining a consistent family history.

Rarely does anyone leave this world without being touched by some malady, or catastrophic illness. My life's journey embraced a long struggle with cancer. I was late discovering my illness, the prognosis after initial examination indicated advanced stage terminal. God knew His will and purpose for permitting that condition to envelope my body. My doctors were treating me on the knowledge they had at hand. I did not know, and neither did the doctors know; the plan God had, to use my suffering to his glory. After a prolonged time of lingering at the threshold of death, I was healed of the cancer. I cannot explain that healing, however, I learned, the weaknesses of our infirmities in no way over shadows the power, and strength of our spiritual character; nor can our outward physical limitations, silence our inward God supplied, life force. Having such truth shown me by Divine mercy, I eagerly share the experience of that revelatory journey.

It has led me to Spiritual places I could never have known on my own knowledge, or strength. It has led to deeper levels of faith, and trust, I never knew existed. The intensity of that trust; has seared into my spirit, an intimacy with God that is impossible to achieve with man. My experience with catastrophic illness has been most instructive to my life, and my spirit. It helped me make the connection between flesh, and Spirit, and to know who rules both.

My life's journey is divided into three great divisions. The first was Preparation which began in the United States Army. I enlisted early, before finishing high school. My record of school achievement up to that point was non-existent. Nothing in my life before the military had been able to jolt me enough to kick start my interaction with personal development. Military discipline, and motivation helped me to realize every deficiency existent in my persona. I had the good sense, with that help, to find, and develop my strengths. For the first time in my life I began to know my real self. I saw a young man of sound intelligence, with a new found confidence, to accomplish anything he desired.

Preparation, took on an urgency I had never known before. Applying for every training program available, I developed skills, and knowledge. Reading became my one of my highest priorities, and, as I excelled, I came to the attention of my superiors. These applications earned me promotions, and greater opportunities to advance. Four years of discipline, training, and travel closed the gaps that my pre-military years had opened. After my tour of duty, I picked up where I left off, and finished High School. My studies continued on to Undergraduate School, Graduate School, and Seminary.

The second division of my life journey was the Ministry. While in the Service, the Holy Spirit confirmed in me, my calling, and election to preach the Gospel. From my earliest cognition, there had been an unrelenting knowing, that I should preach the Gospel. When I was very young, I could not discern what it was that kept transmitting to my whole being. As I grew older, it became clearer. I knew there was no other choice than to be obedient to that call. I studied to show myself approved, and allowed the Spirit to do the rest. I began Preaching and to Pastor immediately after my discharge from the Army. My ministry continued for the next thirty years parallel to my career as an Educator. Even since retirement from Teaching and Educational Administration, my Ministry continues.

The third and last division of my life's journey was the thirty years of Teaching and educational administration. Over twenty of those years were serving as a Principal, and Evaluator/Supervisor. Over the combined years of all my work, I honored the requirements of my employers in each field. As I did, I justifiably told myself I was doing "ministry." I felt so, because all that I learned; in perfecting those divisions of work, and service was spent on teaching, and spreading the Gospel. All through this book are examples, and illustrations of what it takes for any person of normal ability to succeed. I choose to intertwine all of my gifts, and graces into one great effort of giving to others, all that God had given me. There is inspiration here to be gleaned, and absorbed. I hope it will be useful in helping to nurture the young, and to motivate lives desiring another chance. May these precious life gleanings, from six decades of living, be of value, to many readers of this book?

TABLE OF CONTENTS

ACKNOWLEDGEMENTS

The very essence of this book is about inspiration; on my journey I have received more than I can ever give back. If per-chance, you shared with me, some grace, or just a nudge, thank you! I am also indebted to that innumerable passing parade of individuals, especially children, whom I saw, slipping helplessly through the cracks of life. The urgency of my desire to be inspirational came from their plight.

I wish to thank my wife, Annie for her quiet patience, and deep faith, in what I was seeking to accomplish. She was my partner, during my late night writings.

Carol Sullivan provided untiring technical assistance; and in-exhaustible knowledge of media and machines.

My granddaughter Mi' Lisa, from a baby, loved my stories. The encouragement she shared was constant, and priceless.

My sister Lilly, an accomplished author in her own right; spent many hours editing, and giving technical support.

My niece Joy, for her unrelenting encouragement when I was at a stall, I also thank Joy for the editorial, and organizational skills.

Thanks to my brother Michael, for his Prayers, and his encouragement.

Thanks to my friend James Eddy Phillips for being a fan.

Dr. Colbert Whitaker, my unwavering friend, was on board early on. He listened to my ramblings trying to take shape. His patience and encouragement is deeply appreciated.

CHAPTER ONE

FAMILY BEGINNINGS

I was born into the world on that twenty-seventh day of April in 1935. They said I looked so much like my Daddy that my Mother gave me his name, Andrew. In birth order I was the third of their ten children. All of them born at, Meharry/Hubbard Hospital, in Nashville, TN. Before me, my brother Theodore, the firstborn, my sister Mary the second born. Following her were sisters; Addie, Lilly, Cassandra, Carolyn and Hilda. Finally my second and third brothers Michael and James were born. James was the tenth and the last child born.

By virtue of parental DNA each of us received our gifts, and graces of parental likeness, and attributes. Destiny gave each of us a journey uniquely tailored to our individual personas. This writing gives me a very special opportunity to share my journey. So, I start with as much as memory gives me from that April day that I yelled, when I was smacked on my bottom, into earthly reality.

My parents were an unlikely couple. Daddy was born in 1895, and was fourteen years older than mother, who was born in 1909. In 1927 he and Mother had met when he was thirty–two years old. Mother had recently graduated from High School. At age fifteen she had been uprooted by the death of her mother, and the remarriage of her Father. His new marital arrangement, left Mother no choice, but to go to live with her older married sister. By age eighteen, she was very much on her own. Daddy and Mother were introduced by mother's hairdresser, who was daddy's sister,

1

Allie. After they met, Daddy was in hot pursuit, encouraged by his sister. Their courtship thrived, and after a year, they were married.

Their family grew, as the years went by, from one to ten children, born about eighteen months apart. Daddy and Mother seemed happy, however, times were intensely hard. Like many others they were trying to survive the Great Depression. The Depression began in 1929 when the New York Stock Exchange crashed. People made runs on the banks to withdraw their monies. Thousands of businesses failed. Thousands of wealthy, Americans lost their entire fortunes, sending the economy into a tailspin. Across the nation, many jobs were lost. Average poor people, as well as, whole families were caught in the dismal cycle of desperation, hunger, and homelessness. The cycle continued until the year 1939. I was too young to understand the full implications of the depression years. The impact the period had on my life continues to be telling, as I remember the lifestyle my parents were forced to adopt. They would have loved to have been able to do all the things that contributed to a healthy habitat for their children. The grip of poverty forced them as it did many others to a sacrificial bare bones existence. There are good things that come from every situation. I believe the family character was shaped for the better by that lifestyle. The resilience we developed came from our struggles. And indeed, the faith we embraced came from the hope we held that better times would come.

Honesty forces me to recognize, my parents were poor before the Depression. However, I wonder how we would have turned out had our circumstances been favorably different. I happily accept those circumstances under which I was born, even the World War 11, period that makes for such a unique place in history. Had not all of those things been in place, I would not be the person I am. Neither would I have my own unique perspective of those times. There would be no stories for me to tell my grandchildren.

THE SCOVEL STREET HOUSE

My awareness of my individuality came when I was about four years of age. It started when I began to think independently from my family. Until that time, all of my thoughts were in response to the commands of my parents. Awareness came with my fascination of nature, and things beyond our house and yard. We lived in North Nashville on Scovel Street between sixteenth, and seventeenth avenues. Scovel Street was the street north of the main thoroughfare, named Jefferson Street.

Our house was located on the upper end of the block of houses numbered in the sixteen hundreds. The street number was sixteen, sixteen. The house was a Double Tenement, with a built up front yard about two feet higher than the sidewalk. The front porch was three feet higher than the yard. Our tenement side was on the right, facing the house. A wooden swing hung from the porch ceiling held by metal chains. When I got up on that swing, I thought I was on top of the world. Looking out across the yard, and on across the street and beyond, I could see the back of those houses that were on Jefferson Street, that busy thoroughfare.

The entrance to the house was up the concrete steps from the sidewalk, onto the concrete walkway leading to the eight wide wooden steps. The steps led up to the wooden porch that stretched across the front of the house. The door to the tenement was in the middle of the wide porch. Inside that door were two doors; one on the right and the other on the left. My family's tenement side was through the door on the right. It was the entrance into the front room. This room was Daddy and Mother's bedroom, as well as the family gathering place. It had a fire place with a hearth built on the floor under the grate which held the live coals.

In the winter, after supper, the family gathered in a semicircle around the grated fireplace. Huddling together, we watched the black lumps of coal burn, bubble, and hiss, as they became red hot coals, then white ashes. The heat from the fireplace was hot on the front of our bodies, and faces. Behind our semicircle, the room was cold, and we could feel it on our backs. Before adding new lumps of coal, Daddy with his poker would break up the burned coals and ashes. He poked them through the grate allowing them to fall on the hearth below.

Sometimes Daddy would make a hole in the hearth ashes, and place uncooked sweet potatoes in the opening of the ashes. He would then cover them with hot ashes. After a time they would bake. When pealed, what a family treat it was to share and eat those potatoes. That winter family ritual was almost sacred.

As evening wore into night Daddy would be the first to slip from the group, and go to his bed directly behind the family circle. He made a striking figure in his long johns, as he pulled his legs into the bed; while pulling up the covers in the same motion. Daddy needed the rest, and sleep, because he left for work at four o'clock every morning. Next the girls were off to the middle room to bed. Theodore and I lingered by the fire until, Daddy raised up on one elbow, and told us to go to bed. We hated to go upstairs to our dreadfully cold bed room.

The next room was the middle room, in the center of the floor stood the Warm Morning Heater. It stood four and a half feet high. The round belly was heavy sheet metal, which turned red hot when the stove was operating at peak temperature. At front bottom, there was a large rectangular door for draft, and removing ashes. Top front, was another large door to receiving coal. Inside were the ceramic girdle, and a grate. Behind, top was where the stove pipe was attached; it ran to the chimney in the wall behind the stove.

The last room was the kitchen, there stood the six legged cooking stove. It had six iron caps on the top called eyes. Other kitchen furnishing were, a porcelain topped table, a standing old fashioned four legged ice box; and a tall cabinet which held flour, meal, and various seasonings. On the left wall past the stove, was the crude zinc sink, with cold running water. At the back of the kitchen, on the left, was the door to the dreaded bathroom. It had no lights, heat; or hot water. On the extreme right, was the door leading out of the kitchen to the back porch. Here, Mother did the family washing in the number ten wash tub. It sat on a flat table, and had no ringer, only a washboard.

The kitchen stove was essential to our Saturday night bath ritual. The water for the baths was heated in tall lard can on top of the stove. The tub Mother washed clothes in was placed in the middle of the floor. We children were lined up, and bathed one by one; the older children bathing the younger ones. The one drying towel was ringing wet by the end of the ritual. Out of the tub, ignorantly happy, we stood on our toes on the wet, worn, linoleum floor. Smelling like octagon soap we waited for our clean "nighties".

MY PERSONAL NOTES ON THIS CHAPTER

CHAPTER TWO

BUILDING MY WORLD

In 1940, I was five years old; my world was no bigger than our house, the yard, and our street, Scovel. We had no television or other types of media. Scovel Street was a quiet, residential street. The people were older, middle class teachers; professors, and business owners. How my Daddy managed to get us there is still a mystery to me. He was not a trained professional, however, his presence, and manner said differently.

The street over from Scovel was Jefferson. Sitting on the big swing on the front porch caused my imagination to run wild. I would look out across the yard, and on beyond the houses towards Jefferson Street. It sounded very exciting. My eyes were focused on the back of the houses on Jefferson. Looking between each house, I could see the Jefferson Street traffic, zipping by. There were cars, trucks, buses, horse and wagons. My curiosity was, excited by the hum, din; and the rumble of wagons on that busy cobblestone thoroughfare. It was more than I could digest. My imagination was out of control, trying to fathom, what was it was like, up there on Jefferson Street.

Those preschool years were sweet and, carefree. I loved to play outdoors. The front poach was my area. When mother was outside, she permitted me to play down on the yard. On, or off the poach, I was busy in my head, savoring the cloud patterns, or watching the shade line as it fell like a curtain across the trees, and the houses. I loved the way the sun played in the tree leaves, as the wind blew. Nature was so mysteriously beautiful, and I had to provide my own answers to the many questions posed in my head. There were three other children, yet, I lived in my head, as though I was the only child. Still I had good relationships with my brother, Theodore, and my sisters; Mary, and Addie

After supper, my job was to clean the glass lamp chimney of the coal oil lamp. We did not have electricity. Daddy did not allow me to trim the wick, or pour the coal oil into the bottom chamber of the lamp. I was very careful when cleaning the glass chimney with old news papers. Yet, I had to be sure, that all of the soot inside of the glass was gone. Daddy and Mother stressed responsibility, as well as thoroughness. Daddy spoke gently until I understood what was expected, while Mother spoke more harshly. I often had to sneak and cry from my hurt feelings when Mother gave instructions. So while being very careful with the chimney, I hurried in order to go outside and play in the dusk dark of the late evening.

I loved that surreal look that seemed to be, the dividing line between day and night. It was then, that the screeching noise of the cicada began to rise, and grow louder by degrees. The late evening dew brought dampness to the grass, and a cooler atmosphere replaced the warmth of the day. By this time the sun had completely dropped below the horizon. I, my brother, and sisters were ready to start the beloved games we played at night on the sidewalk.

The lone street light, across the street, provided a strange yellow light on the sidewalk where we played. Our favorite games were: High Spy, Momma May I, Dodge Ball, Red Light, Hop Scotch; and It. Sometimes we told stories. Daddy and Mother would often sit on the swing that hung from the porch ceiling, and watch us play.

Other nights, we would chase fireflies. When we got enough of them in a small jar, they would provide a small amount of phosphorus light. A fun thing was to tie thread to the back legs of the June bugs we had caught earlier that day. The string would be about two   feet long. Holding one end of the string, we released the end tied to the June bugs. They would fly in a circle as far as the string allowed, and we turned in the direction they flew.

One of our favorite past times, was to play grocery store in the yard space between our house, and the house next to ours. The fun part was to make the long walk down the graveled alley at the end of our back yard. It   extended down the whole block past the back of each house. It was always clean, and at the end of each yard was what was called, "the dump". Every dump was neatly policed to preserve community pride. Each week the city refuse trucks would come down the alley. The workers, with shovels, scooped up refuse from each dump, and pitched it onto the moving truck.

In the evenings, before we children were called for supper, we would make our pilgrimage down the alley. Our house was the third house from the corner, and that gave us more than two dozen dumps, from both sides of the alley; to pick choice items for our mock grocery store. We looked for meal, and flour bags, we filled them with dirt to make them look full. We looked for empty vegetable cans that had their labels still intact. They were washed, and lined up on the makeshift shelves. Our "turnip greens" was freshly pulled grass. We tried to make our mock, store appear to be as well stocked; and as neat, as the real grocery store across the street from our house. For money we used drink bottle tops with their edges beaten down. We made our paper dollars from cut out paper. The mock store gave us many hours of pleasure.

One evening, after supper, we were on one of our "shopping" trips down the alley, when I made the first really bad judgment of my young life. On one of the dumps, was a clump of white gauze. It was swollen with a red wet substance. In my inexperienced thinking, I thought it would serve as the "fresh meat", for the store. My brother and sisters were as ignorant as I was, and did not object. We placed "this thing", in the empty cellophane lined meal bag, and took it home. Next morning, we could hardly wait until breakfast was over, to go, and set up our store. I made the mock meat cage to look as realistic as possible. The sanitary napkin was placed on a piece of tin, garnished with fresh grass. I sneaked into the kitchen, and went into the ice box. With the ice pick, I chipped a lump of ice off of the twenty-five pound block. An old orange crate, served as the meat display box. A piece of broken glass lay across the front. The display looked pretty good. Everything we used came from the alley. Shortly afterward, Mother came out of the backdoor with her load of washing, to hang it on the outside clothes line. As she came through the yard, passing our mock store, she did a double take look, at our "meat" display. She dropped her washing, and screamed; "who brought this into the yard"? In concert, my brother, and sisters said, "brother, did it"! I received the whipping of my young life. Many years passed, before I understood the reason for my punishment for choosing that item to go in our store. It was my immaturity about the taboo things of life.

BEYOND SCOVEL STREET

The fall of 1942, it was time for me to start school, and I was excited, finally, I was going to see beyond Scovel Street. I was about to experience the things I had been seeing, hearing, and imagining. Mother took me to school that first time. We left the house; and walked to the corner, turned south onto Seventeenth Avenue; headed toward Jefferson Street. We came up beside the rock wall, at the corner of Seventeenth and Jefferson. With bulging eyes, and a pounding heart, there it was, Jefferson Street. It was a whole new unimaginable world, bustling with people; vehicles, and businesses. Mother nearly pulled my arm out of socket as we crossed the street. Heading east, we passed Thompson's Cleaning and Pressing Shop. As we passed, there were two long pipes jutting out of the wall of the building. They hissed streams of scalding steam into the air. All this, far exceeded what I had imagined. My heart raced with excitement, as we headed towards Perkins store on the corner. There, we would turn the corner and head south towards the school. As we approached Perkins Store, we had to navigate through the fifty pound sacks filled with potatoes, the bushel baskets of turnip greens; and the cages of live chickens. These items were on the sidewalk in front of the store. Making the turn off of Jefferson on to Sixteenth Avenue, we walked one block at a time. We crossed many intersections through the east-west streets. We crossed Meharry Boulevard, Phillips, Warren and Jackson streets. Now, we had to go through the vast, new Andrew Jackson Courts. With wide eyed amazement, I walked beside my Mother until we had passed through the Courts, on past Pearl Elementary school. The next street was Herman, and there on the west corner, was the Head Annex Pre-Elementary School. Mrs. Frazier was my first teacher.

THE WAR YEARS

The years of the early forties found America deeply mired in World War II. On the home front, many families, schools, and institutions joined in the war effort. Many Schools held contest to see which could collect the most recycled resources. The children brought mashed tin cans, and bundles of used newspapers. I tried to understand the meaning of those red rationing coupons, and the pennies made of zinc to preserve copper. The government needed the copper to use in the manufacture of aircraft. Things were not explained to children, and slowly; I began to understand how serious the times were. People openly complained about the scarcity of items such as butter, meat, and nylon stockings. When my Daddy one day brought home horse meat for mother to cook, it all began to be very clear. America had entered the war just as the depression was ending. Everyone we knew was having hard times, just as we were.

There were signs everywhere, encouraging enlistment into the Armed Services. There were posters of soldiers posing with their guns at the ready. Other pictures showed an older distinguished man with a little white goatee. Visually, it seemed as though he was pointing directly at the viewer. He wore a red, white, and blue Top Hat; a blue top coat. His shirt was white with a black bow tie. His trousers were red, and white alternating stripes. The caption beneath his picture read Uncle Sam Wants You! This little man, dressed in the colors of the flag, was the Military's official recruiting mascot.

Other signs proclaimed; Buy War Bonds Loose Lips Sink Ships, and Join the Red Cross. The air raids and emergency drills were frightening. We were encouraged to pray, and to trust God. Families who had a person; or persons in the service, displayed a large white star in their window. If they had lost a person in battle, they displayed a gold star. There was one, or several soldier's funeral almost every day. It was sad to see a military car pull up to any home. Everyone knew it was bringing tragic news. To me there was a dreadful pall of unspoken grief, enveloped in patriotism, in the air; however, there were no tears shed. The headlines screamed Hitler's threats daily, they were terrifying. It seemed like any day, the German's would be in Nashville, coming down Scovel Street. I wondered how many other children were terrified by the war, because of the daily ominous headlines.

By 1944, I was nine years old, and in Elementary school. When 1945 came, the war began to turn. As the German Armies fell, the Newspaper headlines screamed of the great celebrations going on in many of Europe's capitols. German strongholds began to fall apart with regularity. By May 1945, news was everywhere that Hitler had committed suicide. His tattered mantel of authority fell to Admiral Doenitz who directed that all German Armies everywhere should surrender to the Western Allies. All hostilities ceased at midnight May 8, 1945. Paris was liberated amid tremendous celebrations and parades. There were news paper picture reports of thousands of French people filling the streets in celebration. The Allied forces marched through the Arch of Triumph in Paris and down the Champs Elyse's. On Armistice Day, November 11, 1945, World War II, was declared to be officially over.

One sad commentary on the war that still vividly comes to mind is the death of President Franklin Delano Roosevelt on April 12, 1945. Our family was grief stricken, as though he were a member of the family. Neighbors were on their porches openly weeping, and verifying the news. The President did not live to see the work he had done to bring peace, come to fruition. President Truman was sworn in to finish out President Roosevelt's term.

At the young age I was, those memories are yet vivid to me. Daddy was a very patriotic individual. He was proud of his status as a Disabled American Veteran of World War l. He had served in the United States Army Calvary, his unit fought in France against the Germans. He received his injuries during trench warfare on the Western Front.

From year to year, he could hardly wait for Armistice Day, celebrated every November. It was his joy to put on his American Veterans of Foreign Wars cap, and take his children to the Armistice Day Parade. It was held at Memorial Square, downtown, Nashville. With his cane, and cap, he stood straight, and at attention. When the soldiers marched by in military formation, Daddy stiffened and smartly saluted, holding it until the unit passed.

MY PERSONAL NOTES ON THIS CHAPTER

CHAPTER THREE

BLACK MANNA AND WINTER SURVIVAL

1947 brought me to my twelfth birthday. My beloved Scovel Street was caught in the grip of a deadly winter. Worry was obvious on Daddy's face. All of beauty and fun of summer, and the colorful fall had passed. Outside, the snowfalls, lay on top of each other. Ice continued to thicken. It was turning out to be a prolonged winter. Everything was scarce. The street had become impassable. There were deep ruts of encrusted, frozen snow, and ice in the tire tracks. Little ridges had formed above the ruts where the wheels had forced mud and snow out. What seemed beautiful to me weeks before, was now, a dirty; ugly brown mush, from many thaws, and freezes. Mud had drudged up from beneath the pavement and sidewalk, and refrozen. I knew that our supply of coal had dwindled down to a few lumps, and shavings. The fire in the front room grate was slowly dying for lack of coal. The middle room, Warm Morning Heater was cooling down because the fire in it had gone out. In the kitchen, white ashes mourned the dying of the fire in the cook stove.

This winter day, with temperature very low, and more snow threatening, Daddy's desperation was obvious. Suddenly, there was a great commotion; many excited voices, outside in the street. They were shrill, and urgent, as people blurted out in unbelief. It was the neighbors, running towards the commotion in the street.

A huge old truck, loaded with coal, had sprawled in the middle of the street. The rear wheels had angled outward from the heavily loaded truck bed. The axel had broken, and the wagon, just sat down in the snow, between its wheels. Big black lumps of coal were all over the ground. The excited neighbors, my brother, and my Daddy were beginning to gather coal with desperate haste. The empty truck bed remained squatted, relieved of its burden, there it stayed until spring came. That blessed infusion of unexpected "BLACK MANNA", lasted our family throughout that winter. I was thankful and was learned how to, "Etch Finger Grips, Into Faith".

LEARNING RESPONSIBILITY

Head School was the Junior High School where Daddy worked. His job was Chief of Maintenance, and Building Custodian. His headquarters was in the Boiler Room, when he was not out in the building. My brother, Theodore, and I called the boiler room Daddy's office. On a daily basis there was always someone seeking his counsel, and wisdom. This included the Principal, and Teachers. I often wondered why the principal was always in Daddy's Boiler Room, rather than his upstairs office.

The building was quite large for one person to be responsible for its maintenance, and cleaning. Daddy's salary was $130.00 dollars a month; as a perk, he was allowed to take home, one huge potato sack; filled with coal each day. He was also given the "ends" of the bread left over from lunches prepared in the cafeteria. The manager carefully put all of the ends back into the bread bags in which they were delivered. At the end of each day the bread would be stacked on the counter for Daddy to take home.

To transport the coal and bread home, Daddy made a wagon in the boiler room at the school. He got material from the junkyard, just past Hadley Park across from the school. The wagon had steel wheels, attached to a makeshift axle; that reached across the bottom of the wagon bed. The wagon was about eight feet long, from front to back. There was a one foot high sideboard around the bed; and a handle across the front end for pushing. He lined the bread bags around the lumpy coal sack, which lay in the middle of the wagon.

For a long time, I thought bags of bread ends could be purchased at the local store. To this day, I prefer to eat the bread ends rather, than the slices between. In truth, daddy was desperately trying to take care of his family. All of this translated to me, how hard it was for impoverished families to survive. Many other families struggling like ours, survived on simplicity, humility; and their finger grips etched in faith.

Next to the Boiler room was the Coal room, both were in the basement of the school. This Coal room was where the coal for the boilers was stored. It was piled high reaching to the top of the room. Daddy moved it to the boiler room with a wheelbarrow. In the Coal room was a large window in the back wall at the very top. The bottom of that window was even with the ground outside. When coal was delivered, the truck backed up to the Coal room window which opened from outside. When the truck bed was raised the coal slid down a chute attached to the truck and fitting in the window. It fell on top of the pile in the coal room. During the day light hours, sunlight streamed through the window. The heat of the sun stirred the dust, and particles of coal to movement. The dust particles danced, turned, and twinkled like suspended diamonds. As the sun's rays passed through the coal dust; prisms of lights reflected off the coal particles.

As toxic as the dust was, it was beautiful to see the combination of coal dust particles, and sunlight interacting. Through my young eyes, that peculiar beauty helped cultivate my sense of the beauty, and its possibilities in natural things. In retrospect, I understand now, why Daddy took me from the boiler room to the coal room, whenever he had something of inspiration to share.

Daddy left home long before daylight. He arrived at school early to light the fires in the two huge Boilers. After they heated, he opened the valves which allowed the water to flow through the pipes inside of the boiler. The hot water made the steam that heated the registers throughout the building. He monitored the steam pressure by reading the several gauges of the Boilers. All things had to be ready by the time the faculty, staff, and students arrived for the school day.

I left home on school days, long before time for me to be at my own school. In one arm, my books, and in the other Daddy's breakfast; a mason jar filed with hot coffee, biscuits, and a container of potato hash. Mother also sent food for his lunch. It was necessary to go past my school, Pearl Elementary, to get to Head School, where Daddy worked. After delivering his food, I headed back to my school.

After school, my brother, Theodore, and I went back to Daddy's place of work. We helped him clean the three floors of classrooms. All of the bathrooms on each floor had to be cleaned, and each hall shined with oil mops as wide as we were tall. The stairs had to be cleaned from the top floor, down to the basement floor; on both ends of the building. We dumped the waste paper from each classroom into a huge cardboard box which we pulled from room to room with harnesses. When we got all the paper to the basement, we took it into the Boiler Room. All of the paper had to be laid in the belly of the great boilers and, topped with slivered planks of wood. Many lumps of coal were placed on the planks.

When the building was cleaned and prepared for the next school day; Daddy, Theodore, and I headed out to the schoolyard. There we performed our last chore of the day; the ritual of taking down the United States Flag. It was obvious that this was a responsibility, he took very seriously. Standing before the flag pole, tall and straight; he grasped the two pulley ropes. Very gently, he pulled one side down; and guided the other side up, until the flag was at the level of his hands. He would allow us to hold the front end of the flag, while he released it from the ropes. We carefully folded the flag. We boys proudly followed his instructions. This ritual translated to us, something precious, and sacred about our country. It spoke silent volumes about our Daddy, and the kind of man he was.

In the late evening we, started the long trip home with our load of coal, and bread. Daddy in the middle with both hands on the wooden handle of the wagon. Theodore was on the left side, and I on the right, holding and pushing. The wagon rolled easily on the flat steel wheels, except when going uphill. We crossed Jo Johnston Avenue, and passed through the gates of Hadley Park. We moved diagonally through the park for a quarter mile, on a dirt path. The path led us down the dirt bank to the seventeenth avenue sidewalk. The railroad tracks were a few feet from where we exited the park, and we proceeded to cross.

Next, the Junk yard, filled with shot-up aircraft from the war. Across the street from the junkyard was the Ice Factory. There, ice was manufactured and sold. The ice was made in one hundred-fifty pound blocks, approximately one foot thick. On the one hundred-fifty pound blocks, four one inch saw indentations were made down the blocks on both sides. Similar indentation was made through the middle of the block. To get a twenty-five pound block, an ice pick was used to chip into the indentation on both sides, cutting out, the twenty-five pounds from the larger block.

We crossed another short set of tracks, and then a short trestle. As a small boy, my legs were scalded when I was caught on the trestle as a steam engine passed on the railroad tracts underneath. Approaching Herman Street, we entered the Fisk University campus. Seventeenth Avenue ran straight through the beautiful campus right up to the historic, Livingston Hall building. After we passed the famous Fisk chapel, we took a short cut down beside the chapel, where we again, picked up Seventeenth Avenue.

Now we had one long block before we reached busy Jefferson Street. We crossed the street, and three houses down, we came to the corner, where

Seventeenth Avenue resumed. We turned the corner, two blocks down was Scovel, our Street. There before us was home, and family. The trip was a total of more than five miles. That daily pilgrimage was necessary to our family's survival.

It was my Daddy's best effort, and I marveled at the dignity he maintained, and the character he displayed. Mother on the home front was equally as industrious. She made most of our clothes on her peddle Singer sewing machine. When we children came out of the house, we looked as though we had stepped out of Band Boxes. At the same time she took in sewing, helping the family economy. By the beginning of the 1950's Daddy was totally immobilized by his war injuries. His greatest life joy was watching his children, growing up, and appreciating the wife he dearly loved.

I thought a lot, about the dire state of my family's poverty; however, I was never ashamed. I believe this was because, in our family, there was no atmosphere, or attitude that we were less, or had less than anyone else. There were many other families around equally as poor, or perhaps more so than ours. I resolved to somehow, rise above the deficiencies of my family. There had not been any college graduates in the family, so I had no pattern of experience to follow. I decided, a way to began was, to develop a personal work ethic, which I would make become my reputation. Through a long succession of jobs, I made it a point to do the finest work possible. I did become known for my good work ethic.

The 1950'S brought new realities to me about my future. The family was growing. We moved from Scovel to Jefferson Street. The move was temporary until an opening came available in Public Housing. Daddy was falling ill more often. His war injuries kept him confined in the veteran's hospital on a regular basis. God, alone, knew what Mother was enduring with teen agers, pre-teens, a sick husband; and little money.

INDEPENDENCE

Work was no stranger to me, it kept me from going home, and the money helped the family. Since age eight I had been honing my work skills. My first job was delivering groceries. My brother, and I, started an ice delivery route. In the summers we cut grass with our push mower, and hand cycle. I learned how to press clothes at a local dry cleaning shop. My friend John got me a job at the Barber shop, shining shoes. Later, he introduced me to the local Pharmacist. I worked at his drugstore, delivering prescriptions. There were many other jobs. One of the hardest, most unpleasant of jobs, was on the "septic truck". This job was cleaning outdoor toilets. The truck was called the honey wagon. It was on this job I began to see the value of an education.

The Korean War was now making big headlines. My brother, Theodore joined the One Hundred and First Airborne Division. Soon after his training, he was sent to Korea. I remember when the family received notice that his division, had parachuted behind enemy lines. Theodore was a highly decorated Korean Veteran. His monthly allotment check helped our family make ends meet. Daddy had become totally disabled.

The money I earned helped the family, although, it seemed there was never enough. This caused me great anguish, but, I did not discuss it with anyone. School was a low priority on my list of concerns. I was not excelling, and I could not understand why. At the time, I did not realize, that what I was feeling was, my mother's oppressive burden of pressure. It was 1952, and Theodore would soon be discharged. This led me to make a life altering decision.

A MILITARY WAY OUT

I decided to join the Army, at the same time Theodore was getting discharged. My enlisting would allow my family to continue receiving the military allotment. It also saved me from being a complete school dropout. It was 1953, and I was a senior in High School. I struggled all summer with the issue of what to do about school, knowing I was not going to graduate. That September, I enrolled and attended for three days. It was during those days that I finalized my decision to quit school. My Mother was devastated by my decision. She desperately wanted me to continue in school. For the first time in my life, I was adamant. Finally, my Daddy, who never had overruled my Mother, said, "Althea, Let the boy go".

Except for a summer in Chicago in 1952, I had not been outside the State of Tennessee. On September 5, 1953, at age eighteen. I took the oath to join the United States Army at the Federal Building in Nashville. Immediately after taking the oath, I and two other inductees were flown to Columbia, South Carolina. From there we were driven to Fort Jackson, (Tank Hill), to begin basic training. The Reception Center was a nightmare as we were herded into processing lines. We were ordered to strip, and our bodies were inspected, measured, and sanitized. Our heads were shaved completely. We were issued military clothing, boots, and gear. Eventually, we were issued a rifle, and a service manual.

It took a while to understand the hostile way the cadre gave instructions. Their loud harsh commands did not mean they were angry, they were essential. It was essential to the training process. After I figured that out, taking orders was not a problem, but the abuse brought me to tears. It was obvious, that I had a lot of growing up to do. I decided, the way to survive was to bury my sensitivity. I would do this by steeling myself to everything external to my persona. That attitude helped me decided to be one of the best soldiers the Army could make. There was a lot to learn, and I quickly sized every opportunity to excel in soldiering.

At Fort Jackson's 'Tank Hill," Basic Training began, drilling, marching, running, and studying; day and night. The training involved much more, and continued for eight weeks. Kitchen patrol, and guard duty was constant. There were classes on map reading, close combat with bayonets, and mock wars between companies. These exercises were highly competitive, and intense. We all were amazed, as we turned from boys to soldiers. We marched on the base parade field days on end, we were marching for precision. One day late in our training, the company looked and moved like one instrument. The South Carolina sun, sand, and insects were relentlessly cruel. Finally, it was time to graduate, December, 1953. A list was posted, naming those who had passed basic training. It detailed new orders, and assignments. With graduation came my first promotion, Private First Class. My orders gave me a thirty day leave, after which, I was to report to Fort Eustis, Virginia.

MY PERSONAL NOTES ON THIS CHAPTER

_____

_____

_____

_____

_____

_____

_____

_____

_____

_____

_____

_____

_____

_____

_____

_____

_____

_____

_____

_____

CHAPTER FOUR

THE RIDE HOME

I left Fort Jackson, by Greyhound Bus, feeling like I had been gone for an eternity. In reality, only four months had passed. Those months made a great difference in me, mentally, and physically especially. I was lean, and muscular, and very confident. The nation was locked in the grip of a transportation strike. The only mode of travel was the greyhound bus. I boarded the bus at Newport News, Virginia. The trip from Virginia to Nashville was a long ride. In spite of being in uniform during wartime, Southern "Jim Crow" laws required me to go to the back of the crowded bus. It smelled of urine, and feces, and my seat was next to the toilet. I felt humiliated, and angry. Savoring my newly learned discipline, I resolved not to allow external circumstances to rob me of my dignity. I held on to my duffle bag, and endured the indignities. Concentration helped me hold my bladder, and calm my stomach. The big Hound rolled down the line, thrusting into the Virginia countryside, and the night. Every stop was like another nail of humiliation, and indignity being driven by Segregation. Many of the facilities at the stops denied Black persons entrance. Stopping at Richmond, Lynchburg, Roanoke, Bristol, Kingsport, Johnston City, Jonesboro, and on down the line to Knoxville. Rolling hard, yet stopping at stores, post offices, and every other rural destination between the larger cities. Other stops were Sweetwater, Athens, and Cleveland.

Many things helped take my mind off my immediate problem. I felt good, and I was proud as I reviewed all the changes I had undergone in four months. The person I was when I left Nashville was transformed. The new me was sporting a new confidence, new goals; a new attitude. For the first time I felt that I could achieve anything I desired. While the military was a hardening process by its nature, it gave back big benefits. For me, the Army did what public school undid. All my years in public school had been demoralizing and sometimes depressing. I decided if one did not enter school with built in confidence and status. The danger of school being an unpleasant experience was greater. This was especially so for children from impoverished environments.

The Army takes a person, accesses all of their capabilities. They then placed that person in training areas that complement their intelligence. Great concentration is put on developing the body to its highest degree of operating potential, and strength. The combination of all of that working together brings out character, and leadership. After eight weeks, this is what the Army was sending home in me. Twelve years of school had never touched any of that potential. Those were the thoughts that became my companions, as I sat on the back seat of the Grey Hound bus, next to the toilet.

A DAY IN CHATTANOOGA

After riding nearly sixteen hours, the bus arrived at Chattanooga, TN. The city was unattractive, dirty, and polluted. The Grey Hound rolled in on track five. The driver announced there would be a five hour layover before going on to Nashville. I did not know a single soul in Chattanooga, and I wondered how I would spend so much idle time. The station was crowded, and dirty. Nashville, and home, flooded my thoughts.

After using the fetid smelling restroom, outside seemed the best option for a place to wait. Leaning against the wall in front of the station, my eyes swept Chestnut Street. I looked south towards Lookout mountain, then north towards the Tennessee River. I thought, maybe I'll walk around the city, but saw no welcoming direction to start. The pollution was insufferable. I stood leaning on the fence, then sitting on my duffle bag. Here I was, stuck in this ugly, rambling city, longing for home. What a miserable day of my precious leave, wasted. How could I have known that, years later, I was to return to Chattanooga, spin a career, raise my family, and retire, calling it home.

How strange is Destiny and Fate, in spite of the pre-conceived thoughts of humans? These forces work their own plans for persons and things. Over the years, Chattanooga has morphed into one of the most beautiful cities in the nation. Industries have met clean air standards, citywide beautification has replaced blight, and historic districts have been created. The river walks, and greenways are unique, and beautiful. Downtown is a Mecca for tourism, and the art district continues to revitalize an area once thought hopeless.

In retrospect, neither I, nor Chattanooga really chose each other. Those two forces mentioned above put us together that day in 1954. They ignored my intense rejection, and had her to offer me a livelihood when other places I choose turned me down. Over many years, how good we have been for each other. I taught her children, and she fed mine.

MY PERSONAL NOTES ON THIS CHAPTER

_____

_____

_____

_____

_____

_____

_____

_____

_____

_____

_____

_____

_____

_____

_____

_____

_____

_____

_____

_____

CHAPTER FIVE

THE RIDE INTO MANHOOD

My thirty days of leave was over, I left Nashville in January of 1954, for Fort Eustis, Virginia. As the bus rolled further, and further away from home; all I could think, was how much I was already missing home, family, and friends. During my time on leave, my church had taken on a new dimension of meaning in my life. I now know, this was because at the time; I was keenly feeling my ministerial calling.

I actually could, for the first time in my life, distinguish between blood family ties, and friendship/social ties. Two years before going into the Army I had met Annie, and fallen hopelessly in love. Those weeks of corresponding during basic training had sealed our relationship. We had decided to be married; having to leave her was truly heartbreaking.

The bus rolled on to Knoxville; on up to Bristol, and crossed the State line into Virginia. Every mile, was an emotional roller coaster. I thought of my leave, the Army, my girl; the strange aloneness, and the new realities. All these thoughts told me, I had made the transition from boy to man. The bus reached Richmond, rolled down to Newport News, Virginia. From there, to my destination, the Army base, Fort Eustis, Virginia. Here I would begin a new phase of my life.

1954 was a significant year in America, especially for the Military. President Eisenhower issued a Presidential Proclamation. All Military installations were to be integrated immediately. There would be no more segregated barracks, training, or facilities in any of the Services. At my new assignment, Fort Eustis, Virginia, racial tensions ran high in the barracks where I lived. Upon arriving at Fort Eustis, the living arrangements in the barracks, were, Whites on one side of the barracks, and Blacks on the other side. Then, BAM! The Presidential order came without warning. No segregated sides. Each double bunk bed was to have; a White soldier, and a Black soldier. Immediately, there was open talk by both races of resistance to the change. Mostly, it was hard core White soldiers who did not want to be mixed with Blacks soldiers. Now there was no way around the order to mix. Black/White in each set of beds down both sides of the aisle. There was talk of getting guns, and there were fights. Company Commanders, the Military Police, and Platoon Sergeants; quickly put down the rebellion by threatening Court Martial's, Prison terms, and Dishonorable Discharges.

I had no problem with mingling with White soldiers, or sleeping in a bunk bed with White soldiers. Realizing the historical significance of this order, and how important it was for the country, I was happy to do my part to help make the order work. After many months, things started to settle down. By 1955, Black and White soldiers served side by side; slept, and ate together,   and forgot it was ordered by the President.

In spite of being raised in a poor family, there were virtues taught that no amount of money could purchase. It made me proud that my parents never taught their children there was any difference between Black, and White people. Their mantra was…to love all people, and treat them with respect. This gave me an advantage many soldiers did not have, because my value system was not poisoned by preconceived racial prejudices.

GETTING DOWN TO BUSINESS

I immediately began the arduous training for oversea duty on the continent of Greenland. My first classes were on arctic clothing and survival. Next, I had to learn all about climate, and the culture of the continent, especially of the Eskimo people. My manhood was not the only thing changed, I had developed a new appreciation for learning. In grade school, I hated learning, and school, Now, I found learning fascinating. Studying about the arctic terrain was equal to a college geography course.

The most interesting of all the courses was the one on the Aurora Borealis, or Northern lights. Regardless, of what was taught, it did not offset the erratic, ghostly ambience, when I saw them in reality. They stood in the night sky, like giant rings of DNA, in rainbow colors. Without warning, they would take off with lightening speed, erratically twisting, suddenly turning; diving and climbing. It seemed at times they were going to crash at the spot where I stood. The seasons of Greenland were, six months of night, and six months of day. The frigid night season allowed the Northern Lights with their ghostly intelligence; to put on a continuous, eerie light show. In stark silence they whipped, and snapped like the tail of a kite.

The final phase of my training was Stevedore School. The classes were held in Richmond, Virginia at the Hampton Roads Port of Embarkation. I learned all about different kinds of knots, riggings, booms; and hatches. After learning the theory, came the hands on practice. This was done on ships docked at the Hampton Roads Port, at Richmond Virginia. In April of 1954, I finished my training. My company would be shipping out for the long oversea trip to Greenland, vie way of Newfoundland.

THE CROSSING

In disbelief, I stood on the deck of our ship as it sailed past the Statue of Liberty in New York Harbor. Events changed quickly as the massive Troop Ship moved into the open Atlantic. The calm waters became the turbulent Ocean. The waters turned from blue to green. Swells and gigantic waves enfolded the ship. We were literally pitched upward, and the next instant, the ship came crashing down into the ocean. That reminded me of hitting belly busters, when I was learning to swim.

The fifth night at sea, came one of the most violent storms imaginable. Long before morning, soldiers were vomiting throughout the ship. The heads were full, men were on the floors, some had their heads incommodes, while others sat on them, sick at both ends. Most were dehydrated, and too weak to get off their bunks. They cried, and called for their momma's. I was sick from seeing so many sick men. Whenever possible, I went to the deck; the frigid air numbed me against the nausea. The smell below deck was unbearable, and seasickness was epidemic.

RESCUE

The next announcement coincided with the ship newspaper's lead story. The ship had hit an iceberg and was temporarily disabled. While in repair, the Atlantic Ocean was frozen for miles out to sea. The next announcement told us, an Ice Breaker from New York was being sent to rescue us from the ice. It would take seven days for it to reach our ship. We had been on the water twenty days. One morning, while on deck I noticed a plume of trailing black smoke in the distance. The Ice breaker was coming to free the ship from the icy grip of the Atlantic. The big ship cut through the ice, past our ship, and moved in position in front of us. After a while, our ship began to creak, and moan as it moved in the path created by the breaker. The ice in the ocean was reported to be five feet thick.

We followed for days until we came to the Port of St John's, Newfoundland on day thirty. This place was mysterious, fog drifted around the ship. It seemed the houses were layered on the side of a great rock. Each level was higher, and the fog thicker. None of the soldiers were allowed off of the ship. We were just there to be resupplied for the last leg of the trip. Most of the men appeared to be feeling better.

Finally, the ship's horn bellowed and it began to move. Our next Port was to be Labrador, then on to Greenland. After forty horrendous days on the ocean, we arrived at our destination. Our base was on the D.E.W. LINE (DISTANT EARLY WARNING), only ninety miles from Russia. We arrived in mid-May and furiously worked, unloading, and loading supplies. These were supplies of every kind. By July of 1954 we were ready to return to the States.

CHAPTER SIX

UNFINISHED BUSINESS

The year 1956 was one of the most significant years of my life. So many events were proving to be life changing. I saw these events were going to be the guy wires which would hold many of my life goals. I was discharged from the Army August 26, 1956. The first major thing I did was to enroll in the school I left in 1953, Pearl High. October came, and I did the second major thing. On the seventh of that month, I married the love of my life, Annie. I was twenty-one and sharply focused on what I had to do to insure a solid life. Plunging into work, school, and ministry, I was possessed with a motivation, and drive I had never experienced before. There was so much I had to catch up on, before qualifying for graduation. After eighteen months I graduated on June 5, 1958. My wife Annie knew how important this was to our future. This importance was enhanced by the birth of our first child, Sebrina. She was cuddled in Annie's arms at my graduation ceremony.

PUTTING ON THE HATS

On Monday June 8th, I enrolled in the Freshman Class, at Tennessee State University in Nashville. Plunging into college studies and, avoiding the social amenities of college life. As a mature veteran, I knew what I wanted, and where I wanted to go. We lived off campus, and when I did not have classes, I was working. On weekends I was preaching, and serving as an Assistant Pastor. The college years flew by, in retrospect, my studies went very slow. To my surprise, my grades were exceptional, and instead of keeping up, I lead the class. Concurrent to college work, I was doing a Ministerial Ordination Study Course for my church. I finished the course work in 1957. Excelling in the Church's requirements, I passed the Board of Examiners and qualified for Ordination. I was ordained at the National Annual Convocation in Nashville, Tennessee, August 1957.

TANGIBLE PROGRESS

My college graduation was in May of 1962.The hard work and study was paying big dividends. I received the Bachelor of Science in Sociology Degree. My minor was History, with Certification for teaching. At the graduation Annie was holding our second child, Andrew, he was one month old.

Foundational to those years of college, and study was my military training, and travel. Had I not gone into the service it is doubtful I would have ever known my true potential. I would not have had the confidence to have finished High School. What would have been my contributions to society, and the world?

These issues are important to revisit because, I was not the last victim of insecurity. During my years of teaching, and my experience as a Principal; I saw so many young lives caught where I was in my pre-military years. I can only wish that every child be guided into experiences that are liberating instead of stifling.

THE SEARCH FOR WORK

After graduation I was sure that finding a job in my field would be easy. After searching, and applying for months, I discovered I was quite naïve about the world of work. Even with all of my travel, and military experience, I was turned down time after time .I must have thought my diploma held magic. Upon presenting it, for employment considerations, I imagined doors would open, and barriers would fall. The hard reality was, they shut tighter, and often, I felt resentment from those I had come too, for help. Several potential employers gave the reason, "too much education". For a year, I had "beat the pavement," searching for meaningful employment. Instead, I found myself, in Hell's Kitchen, busting suds over pots and pans.

Losing faith was not an option, however, fate had me doing another round of menial jobs, to stay honest, and feed my family. It was humbling to do these jobs, and know I had worked so hard to better myself. It was good to have a college diploma, but I learned, an old saying was true; "it's not always, what one knows, sometimes it's who one knows.

The long string of humbling jobs continued: Custodian- Shoe Mold Operator- Pot Washer- Drive-In waiter- Night Kitchen Cleaner-Bell Hop-Janitor and so on. These jobs earned me enough money to sustain my family. The most immediate goal I had was to hang on, until a break came. I knew all of the hard study was not in vain. I was thankful that Annie accepted my goals as her own; even though it required us to live a very sacrificial lifestyle.

DE'JA' VU

I had sent teaching applications to schools systems all over the nation. At last, a letter arrived from the Chattanooga Public School System. My Sister Mary, and her Husband Cordell, lived in Chattanooga. Cordell was a local Church Pastor. The Director of the choir at Cordell's church, was a Principal in the Chattanooga School System. He requested they give me an interview. By that request, the School System extended me an offer to interview for a position as an Elementary Teacher.

My mind raced back eight years, to 1954, as a young Soldier, I had a five hour layover at the Grey Hound Bus Terminal in Chattanooga, trying to get home to Nashville. Little did I realize; I would be returning to Chattanooga as a Teacher, become a Principal; and serve as a local Pastor. After a long career, it was the city, where I would spend my retirement years.

The interview was successful, I eagerly accepted the position. My wife, Annie and our children had sacrificed so much for me to finish school. I was twenty-eight years old. By the fall of 1963, I was on my way to the city I had scanned from Chestnut Street, in 1954. At the time, I saw Chattanooga from biased eyes. They were clouded by my youthfulness, and, the harsh practices of Racial Segregation. It was those very practices that forced me to ride across Virginia on that cramped back seat of a Grey Hound Bus. Across the South prior to the 1960's, those kind of "Jim Crow" laws were strictly enforced. Little did the Nation know how greatly the Civil Rights Movement would change the practices of Racial Segregation in American society?

CHANGING TIMES

Doing work with dignity, that complemented my training, was exhilarating. I taught elementary grades fifth, and sixth. My assignments included language, mathematics; and art. I loved the children, and the challenge of contributing to their education. That November, will be forever etched in my memory. Near the end of the school day, without introduction, we heard the news. It came directly over the radio, vie, school intercom. "The President has just been shot in Dallas, Texas. He is being taken to Parkland Hospital…the President is dead!" It was the voice of the celebrated Commentator, Walter Cronkite. The nation's 35th President, John F. Kennedy had been assassinated. It was Friday, November 22, 1963. The time was 1:30, PM.

MY PERSONAL NOTES ON THIS CHAPTER

_____

_____

_____

_____

_____

_____

_____

_____

_____

_____

_____

_____

_____

_____

_____

_____

_____

_____

_____

CHAPTER SEVEN

PERSERVING THE BINDING TIES

My young twenty-seven years of life had blessed me with a wealth of knowledge, and wisdom. While acquiring all of this, my siblings were also coming into their own. Theodore the oldest, was totally engulfed in pursuit of his career as a musician. Mary, was now married, and engrossed with her family. Addie had married, and moved to Milwaukee.

With my new job, and young family, my plate was full. Though carrying heavy responsibilities, I knew I could not detach myself from the great burden my mother shouldered. Daddy had died in 1959. The four oldest children were making their own lives. However, there were six younger children still at home. Mother had access to me when I lived in Nashville while finishing college. Each day, whenever, I could find time between classes, and working; I went to her house. This ritual allowed me firsthand knowledge, of how she was doing, and it let the children know, she had support. They understood my task was to be the disciplinarian, and Father figure. This arrangement worked very well. Whenever Mother called, I dropped everything, and got to the house. My younger siblings gave me the utmost respect.

When I left Nashville to take my new job in Chattanooga, Mother, and I modified our plan. I went to Nashville every available weekend. Whenever, emergencies occurred, I went immediately. Mother and I kept these arrangements until all of the children were out on their own. A few times, I teased her about marrying again; she would always recoil, and stress her commitment to her children, especially the girls. We together, were committed to seeing the children grown. For years after we were all grown, it was Mother's joy to visit her children, especially, if they were sick, or a grandchild was being born. She was the reigning matriarch of her family until her death, June 10, 1993. She was eighty-four years of age. She left thirty-four grandchildren, thirty-seven great grandchildren; and two great, great grandchildren.

MY PERSONAL NOTES ON THIS CHAPTER

_____

_____

_____

_____

_____

_____

_____

_____

_____

_____

_____

_____

_____

_____

_____

_____

_____

_____

_____

CHAPTER EIGHT

WHEN I SAW THE STOP SIGN

In theory there is a five year corridor to be traveled before one reaches their retirement date. In my own case, I was three years into that corridor before realizing being there. My ability to do formal work, competently, was deteriorating. In the years since retirement I have analyzed the reason I did not see the signs telling me, I could not work beyond two more years. I was in denial, brought on by the momentum of habit, and routine. I had reached the ceiling of my earning capacity, and wanted to enjoy it as long as I could. At the time, my age was fifty-three, running; working, going full speed ahead. I was going at the pace of someone who had twenty more years.

Work is therapeutic, and provides one with a sense of wellbeing. As I analyze my situation, I was simply trying to wear too many hats. It was getting hard to wear them all well. I was the administrator of a large urban Junior High School, and served as the Pastor, and Teacher of a large urban Church. Both positions were demanding, and required tremendous outputs of ability, energy; and attention. My weekends were crammed with counseling, appointments; travel, and preaching. Every day was a crisis oriented challenge.

At school, my days were filled with meetings, conferences, seminars, telephone calls, mail; and appointments. The demands of personal management, and public relations were unrelenting. I had worn my "hats," and met all of those demands for twenty-five consecutive years. Age fifty-five was closing fast, and all of my "hats" suddenly became very weighty. Overwhelmed, I began to feel my inner life force, colliding with the

41

external forces I had inflicted upon myself. These feelings told me I needed to re-evaluate, and make some adjustments. I needed to prioritize things in the order of their importance. Deep within, I felt an intensified pressure that laid these needs heavily on my heart.

THE BREAKOUT OF STRESS

A typical workday started around four-thirty each morning. My routine was a shower, exercise, and a try at talking to Annie through her sleepiness. This was how we coordinated the needs of our children, and our household. After, I made my way to each of our four children's bedside. Lovingly, I would make mental notes of how precious they were to me.

By seven A.M., I was in the school office, preparing for a full round of inspection of the school's facilities. The rounds included mini-conferences with the Cafeteria Manager, the Custodian, and the Lead Teachers. By eight A.M., the tour was finished. My tour of the outside campus was started, then back to the office for the long parade of Parent, and Student conferences. By ten A.M., it was time to make sure the first lunch was prepared, and ready to be served. There was a check to make sure the classes scheduled for first lunch were on time.

Usually there was a meeting or two, off campus. Upon returning to school, I would hold disciplinary conferences. As the day wore on, there was the checking, and the ordering of supplies. Teacher evaluations were on going, and time had to be taken to assist teachers with problems, or complaints. There were always after school appointments, and athletic practices, or games. There were always night games to attend. By ten-thirty, or eleven I would start home. This routine varied from day to day, however, no less intense.

During my twenty years as a Principal, I served three different schools. I was three years into my retirement corridor when the tell tale stress signs began to affect me. My first two children were crossing the threshold of adulthood. The last two were teenagers. During some of their most crisis oriented growing up periods, I was deeply mired in my own personal gridlock, struggling with my male midlife crisis.

RUPTURE

Late into the fourth year of that theoretical five-year retirement corridor, my body began to respond to the burnout my mind was feeling. I felt the heaviness of this breaking, but could not identify what was happening. It felt like a crack was widening in the fabric of my life. One day in the middle of reviewing a large stack of mail, the undoing started. First, my mind slipped out of sync with my eyes. Suddenly, I did not know who I was, or what I was doing at this official looking desk. What was I doing in this room? Strangely, I did not panic, something said, "Just wait". For some indefinite period of time, I was immobilized. Slowly, my brain came in sync with my eyes. And slowly, my true sense of "in the present moment," came back into focus. What was a tare, had become a rupture.

DENIAL

I was back to normal, quickly, I considered all this to be just an isolated incident. As the days passed, I blocked what had happened out of my mind. Disregarding the warning, I plunged into my work in the relentless way characteristic of myself. I continued the long fourteen hour day rituals. My weekends were still filled with traveling, counseling; and preaching. Finally, on my way home one evening, I did not know who I was or where I was going. I stopped my car, and again obeyed the silent command to wait. Shortly, my awareness returned.

Even with these strange episodes I was not connecting the dots. Had I paid attention, I would have known, that, the outward pace of the body's energies; cannot exceed the mental, emotional, and cognitive drivers that are internal. When my eyes, and my brain, stopped communicating, I should have known then, I was in trouble. The only way my body could stop me was to break at it weakest point. Eventually, that is what happened. Could I have done something differently? It becomes clear that God does not cause stuff to happen to us, we do. He does graciously intervene, after we mess up.

THE ZIGZAG CRACK

One evening, my youngest daughter Kelly was delighted to see me home so early. She was eager to talk, and share the little games we loved to play. We also enjoyed after dinner walks through the wooded areas adjacent to our home. On this evening, I was tired, and listless. Conversation was out of the question. I just wanted to crash in my chair. As I sat there enjoying my trance, Kelly said, "daddy, you are not your old self any more, you have changed." Her observation stabbed like a knife in my heart. A wave of helplessness flowed over me like nausea. All of my warnings flashed before me. Now I must take them seriously, before something tragic happens. I thought fifty five is too young to retire. I wanted to go the full length of the five year corridor. Head sense, was directing my outward behavior, some inner voice gave different input. It was the voice of God saying, "Whatever energies you have left, I claim them for myself." I heard, and I acknowledged.

The work world treadmill that had so driven me, finally, came to a stop. I announced my retirement at age fifty-five effective June 30, 1990. My career covered forty-two years. They spoke to all my experiences from the Military through Education, Ministry; and Business. The years of my work, and service had enabled me to build a solid network of relationships. I had engaged with people, from all walks of life. Sharing these resources may prove helpful to someone in the work world.

- The latent powers of positions must be connected to facilities, and resources, rather than ego.
- The hallmark of leadership is one's ability to extend kindness, and goodwill.
- Life is reciprocal, it rewards according to what has been invested.
- Mercy is bountiful, when mercy has been shown.
- Blessings are not sequential; they alternate between trials, and tribulations.
- Goodwill goes further than a gift.

The fruit of true labor is fulfillment, the kind that does not slip through the inevitable cracks of life.

MY PERSONAL NOTES ON THIS CHAPTER

CHAPTER NINE

GRABBING HOLD OF THE ROCK OF FAITH

I plunged into full time ministry after retiring from the School System. My goal was to give the Pastoral Ministry my fullest focus. How could I know, what lay ahead would surpass any challenge imaginable. God was preparing to do a new thing with me. Before retiring, I always said, the many hats I wore were, all ministry. Those years of secular work, mixed with ministry were not always, great test of faith. Neither were they, pure good works. Most times it was a response to the momentum, my work demanded.

My secular job required compromises, and sometimes non-Christian responses to serious conflicts, and challenges. The world of work often presented, the kind of consequences, I was ashamed to ask God to bless. I could only thank Him for His longsuffering love for me, in my errors.

True ministry was demanding that I earnestly pick up the weight, and burden of the Cross of Christ. It required God fearing prayer on behalf of those for whom I made intercession. This real ministry required self sacrifice, and total spiritual commitment. It required real Spiritual power that others could witness in my life. God truly does know how to temper those He appoints, and anoints. I began to understand, I needed His tempering to develop spiritual intimacy. God began grafting these gifts into my being, in His own peculiar way.

THE NONCONSUMING FIRE

My "tempering" took off in high gear, two years out of retirement. One day while using the bathroom, my urine became a solid stream of dark blood. There was no pain, however, the sight, and volume of bleeding, horrified my senses. The doctor immediately put me through a prostate examination. The processing was going to take a week to complete. I decided to keep my planned trip to California on schedule. While there, I refused to give thought, or voice to my dilemma. Up setting my wife; and my son, whom we were visiting, was not necessary.

Upon returning to Tennessee, there was an urgent message waiting, "call your doctor's office immediately". A dreadful premonition crowded my thinking. I called, and was told to come in to see the doctor immediately. The kindly doctor tried hard to soften the harshness of the news. I encouraged him to speak as frankly as necessary. With relief, he said, "Mr. Frierson, you have prostate cancer, and it seems to be in an advanced stage of development." He described the gland as being spongy, and swollen on examination. The doctor tried to be consoling. He said my condition was unusual for a man only fifty-seven years of age. Consciously, I contemplated my mortality, surprisingly, there was no panic. My greatest concern was my wife, and family. My doctor instructed me to inform my wife, and return with her one week from that fateful Wednesday.

I called Annie from Sweetwater, and asked her to meet me downtown in Chattanooga for lunch. She was characteristically delighted. Making my way to meet her, my mind replayed every sermon I had ever preached. Every word of counsel I had given, replayed in my head. It was time now, to apply these wisdoms to myself.

Everything in me now was struggling to get a "Finger Grip" into the "Rock of Faith". Quickly, I learned I could not pray objectively for myself. Unashamedly, I began to seek the prayers of others, and the mercy of God. Annie was waiting as I pulled into the parking area of our selected restaurant. We agreed this place was quiet, and we would be less likely to be known. As we were seated, settling in, a comedy of errors began to unfold. Each time I leaned in to begin the dreadful news, we were recognized by some previous acquaintance. After the first time, we tried again. Suddenly, a dear old friend rushed over; with greetings, hugs, and extended memories of old times. Anger and agony filled my spirit. I felt totally invaded. Afterwards, there were no more interruptions.

48

As I began to spill, Annie sensed my emotional distress. She listened with compassion, displaying emotions of steel. She stroked my arm, and held my hand. When I finished relaying what the doctor had said, our eyes were brining with tears. We resolved to fight, and to never give up.

EXERCISING FAITH

We dried our eyes, finished our lunch, and went back to our jobs. Parting, we knew we had enough love to endure, to give to each other for the journey ahead. Consultations and review of treatment options followed the official prognosis. After many tests, we settled on the treatment option of surgery. This option was based on the result of a sonogram test. It pinpointed the dimensions of the cancer, which appeared to be confined to the prostate area.

It was mid-September, 1992, my surgery, was scheduled for October 12, 1992. For the next four weeks, I went to the blood bank. They took my blood, and stored it to be used during my surgery. Annie, the doctor, and I talked about my prognosis, and our hope for success. I made my will, sealed it and gave it to Annie just before being wheeled into the operating room. The eleventh came on Sunday, and surgery was scheduled for the next morning. That Sunday, I conducted the Church service as usual, including preaching. After service, we drove to Knoxville, where my surgery was to be done. I checked into the hospital, the preparation started immediately.

DEVASTATING NEWS

Early Monday morning I was wheeled into the operating room. Annie and I talked until I went under the anesthesia. The last thing we did was to assure each other of our mutual love. My family gathered to wait with Annie during the surgery. I was glad she did not have to face the devastating news that followed, alone. The cancer had spread from the pelvic region to the lymphatic system; it had metastasized and was declared, inoperable. The Doctor stated the only option was to close the abdominal cavity as quickly as possible.

Upon waking, the first person I saw was Annie; then my mother, four of my sisters, and my daughter Kelly. They were ringed around my bed, silent, and sad. I thought I was dead, and they were viewing my body. After a pause, I asked Annie if they got the cancer. Instead of an answer, a tear fell, and she finally spoke. She reluctantly told me. The cancer had spread so much, it was inoperable. I was speechless, and became sick. We quickly regrouped, and decided to make the most of life, moment, by moment.

There were more consultations, and considerations of options for treatment, to buy time. My Urologist confessed there was nothing that could be done. He advised us to "get our affairs in order" as quickly as possible. We choose the option of radiation upon recovery from surgery. Annie and I did not waver, or whine, or cry. We resolved to hold on to the "Rock of Faith".

Radiation therapy started in mid-November, and treatment was scheduled on a daily basis. The treatment called for forty-three massive doses. The first ten days were easy; the only side effects were headaches, and a mild loss of stamina. My body soon reached its toleration level to the radiation, and it became more difficult to endure. The last fifteen treatments were excruciatingly painful.

My determination was greater than the temptation of resignation. Each day I took great care to groom myself as though I was going to the office. I never failed to read the scriptures and pray to God. Arriving at the hospital for treatment, I went throughout the waiting room greeting other cancer patients. I felt any word of encouragement was important. Many of them thought I was a staff person. The healing, and recovery period from the radiation was slow, and my body knew it had a tremendous battle ahead.

ESCALATION

Radiation doses were massive for seven and one half weeks. Having met the prescribed amount, I graduated from the program. Assuming my progress was on the upswing, the next check revealed my prognosis was getting worse. It had been six weeks since radiation ended. When my urologist examined, he discovered an elevation in my PSA reading, (Prostate Specific Antigen). The reading was up from twenty-five, which was already high, to eighty-one.

The letter came from my primary care doctor, my urologist, and my oncologist. They served as my team, and together issued my latest Pathology report. It read Stage D, Terminal. I was now doing all I knew to do, searching for somewhere, some place to find "Finger Grips in The Rock that is Faith".

Annie was still working, and I was adamant she did not stay at home with me. By the grace of God I continued to get up each morning, and act as though I was going to a Job. That job was praying, crying, and talking to God. I begged for my life by promoting my years of good works to His remembrance. Each day all the mistakes, and ill deeds I had ever done, paraded through my conscience. Strength was waning, and my body was failing. During the day I crawled around outside in my back yard trying to plant spring flowers. I could not find the strength to dig the holes. Rolling over onto my back, and through my tears, and feelings of mortality, I looked up through the canopy of pine trees that gently swayed in the breeze.

It seemed I could hear God screaming at me in anger. His questions were in regard to my sins, and errors. Again, in anguish I begged for my life. The response was, "Why should I spare you?" I cried, "My work for you is not finished, my wife, and family need me. My grandchildren need my guidance, and presence in their lives." There were no answers, I imagined God had gone.

When Annie got home from work, she asked, had I had good day. I told her I thought I was dying earlier, she retorted, why, do you not have supper ready. It is only in retrospect, that I understand, and respect what she was doing. Thankfully, she never indulged me in pity. At my lowest points of suffering was when she was strong and resolute. Later she told me how she would slip away to cry when she had to show that toughness. I am still humbled, when I remember how she begged The Lord, to preserve my life.

MY BODY A BATTLEGROUND

Checkups revealed the radiation had done irreparable damage. Stamina was non-existent, and diarrhea was unrelenting. My flesh was cooked externally in my anal area, and internally in my lower colon. The pain was chronic. Eating was problematic because the lining of my stomach was cooked, causing it to be clinically dead. Each day, new complications, presented themselves. The effect of the cancer, and its attendant problems, differ in each individual. I cried a lot, and learned how to pray earnestly. I sought God through His promises, as Job must have done, during his sufferings. God, in His abundant mercy, let my suffering purge my soul.

I had never allowed my body, soul, and Spirit to hold open dialogue on my mortality. In full health, it always seemed disrespectful, and uncomfortable to even think of mortality. Even reading the daily obituary had been a no, no for me. I now found myself becoming resigned to the possibility, Cancer might kill me. Physically, I felt death's chilly hands flexing to take me. My soul was taking inventory to see if I had a chance for heaven. My Spirit was desperately trying to find something to be cheerful about.

DESPERATION

In consultation with the urologist, he suggested a radical last ditch strategy, an orchiectomy, to stop the flow of cancerous testosterone to the upper organs, and body. We consented to this second surgery in May 1993. Surprisingly, the surgery was deemed to be outpatient. After a four hour observation period, I was dismissed to go home. There was an urgent call waiting from my sister, Carolyn in Nashville. She told me our mother was dying, and wanted me to come immediately. I did not tell her about my surgery. It was Friday, and I felt the weekend would give me some time to heal, and gain a little strength. I told her I would be there on Monday. Mother, over hearing, took the phone, "I may not last until Monday; you had better get on over here."My response was, yes ma'am; dropping everything, I headed straight to Nashville, and to the hospital. Mustering every ounce of determination; I hid the pain, agony; and discomfort, from my family, especially from Mother. She lingered for three weeks, with all of us sharing those last days together. Mother died June 10, 1993. Little did the family know of my agony, and suffering during her Home Going Celebration. Bleeding, in pain, and faint; I felt as though I was dying. God's grace and mercy sustained me through the service.

HOLDING ON

My praying, took on a new tone of humility. I stopped the whining, and the fighting with God. All my spirit wanted to do now, was to beg, Lord, have mercy on me. From my spot on the ground of my back yard, looking up through the canopy of pine trees, I talked to God. In resignation, I yielded, Lord, if you desire me to come home, I am ready, please, allow me to stay.

My Oncologist prescribed Eulexin, to help arrest cancer spread. My Endocrinologist prescribed Estinyl to relive my terrible heat seizures. Without my doctor's approval, I put myself on a regimen of Beta-Carotene, and herbal capsules, including vitamin B-12. Someone told this would help boost my immune system. In addition, I started exercising as much as strength allowed. I was in this fight, not to the death, but to hold on to life.

My brother Michael, a minister, called from Nashville. He called often, to saturate me with long fervent prayers. I was faint by the time he finished praying. Before leaving, he suggested I read the story of Hezekiah in the book of Isaiah, (Chapter-38: 5). Hezekiah was a man whom God had given a death sentence for disobedience. Hezekiah's fervent, penitent, and persistent prayer caused God to reconsider. Hezekiah was extended fifteen additional fifteen years of life.

Hezekiah understood his suffering, but I wondered why mine was so intense. Determined to trust God, I knew He must have been in the process of working something that was beyond my understanding. I knew I had to continue to trust Him, and wait. My temperature shot out of control, and became erratic. A glaze of clammy cold sweet lingered on my body. When the heat waves came over me, my veins constricted, and my, heart pounded as my breath shortened. Nights were miserable because my internal heat drove the perspiration out. At that point the chills caused my body to shudder. Every seven minutes was like beginning death.

Hezekiah's experience was instructive for me. I was inspired to also read the story of Job. Relevant for me in Job's story, was how close he came to death during his suffering. It brought to realization, how, even though the "chilly hand of death" may touch us, only God can grant release from life.

Knowing God's hand was upon me, the complications of multiple treatments were still debilitating. The late nineties ushered in a new string of necessary surgeries. The count was up to seven. The most devastating of all of them, was the double mastectomy. Before starting radiation treatments, the breast, needed to have been irradiated externally, and were not. This caused them to start growing, after I finished the internal radiation. They grew to an enormous size, larger than Annie's. She thought they were beautiful. After a while there was no way to hide their existence. The embarrassment was one of the hardest periods of my life.

THE SUSTAINING POWER OF LIFE

The last three years of the ninety's decade, I struggled to get up, to keep busy; and maintain my sanity. The winter days were the hardest, they were long, and depressing. In order to offset the dreariness, I went through the house, cutting on all the lights. Each morning I groomed as though I was going to work. Spring, and Summers I longingly sat by the window, watching hired men cutting my grass. I so wanted to do myself.

REDEMPTION

The decades, of my first half century, show the 1990's, were the most traumatic, and challenging. They were full of emotions, and physical suffering. As they were closing, it seems they took most of the sorrow they brought. In late 1998 I had finished one my three week checkups. Two weeks later, I received the follow up report of my condition. The letter urgently requested me to return to the doctor's office. With reluctance, I told Annie I was tired of these checkups, and I was not going. She said, "Get ready, put on your best suit, and go.

I arrived, waited, was assigned an examining room. I steeled my attitude to receive any bad news with indifference. The doctor gently knocked on the door, and entered. Holding his clipboard, he greeted me. It was obvious he had some news he did not know how to handle. I said, whatever it is, just tell me." Abruptly, he blurted out, "Mr. Frierson, there is no trace of cancer in your body." He went on to say I would die from something, but it would not be cancer.

I received this news as God granting the request I had made that day in the yard. Complications, continued, they revealed daily wisdom I applied to my life. The heart of that wisdom is the knowledge: that the very essence of life is reconstituted, when forces beyond goodness, try to kill the body. No wonder, The Psalmist David said, (Psalms 139:14), "I am fearfully, wonderfully made."

MY PERSONAL NOTES ON THIS CHAPTER

_____

_____

_____

_____

_____

_____

_____

_____

_____

_____

_____

_____

_____

_____

_____

_____

_____

_____

_____

CHAPTER TEN

BEYOND SEXUALITY

When my illness was discovered, Annie, and I had been married thirty-six years. The adjustments forced us to reevaluate our values, and foundation of all of those earlier years. First, we learned that our love was pure, strong; and grounded in faith. Next, we learned, a good percent of marital relationship is grounded in multifaceted sexuality. In our unsolicited transition, to total abstinence, we relearned how to love for love's sake. It taught us, how to love for the joy, and purity of an agape relationship. The kind, that leaves no room for selfishness, or manipulation. Now it was clear, our relationship needed to be of a greater Spiritual quality, than physical sexuality.

We did begin a new kind of coexistence we had not known before. It is surprising how much easier it is to exist without the life pressure of sex. So many married couples define life itself, and success, by the quality, and content of their sexuality. In spite of having been stricken early (fifty-seven), we had enjoyed a very good life. Now we know why we had married early. We were sexually healthy then, and had no problems in that area. We had our children in our youth, and I played with them all when they were children.

I believe God is involved in the twist and turns our lives take, especially if we intimately know Him. I say this, because, of the wonderful way He has given Annie and I, fullness, at a place we expected to find emptiness. As a young man I remember thinking, "how can a man live without sexual capability." I found the answer, only when I had a desperate need to know.

It was then I found, the quality of life at that place is less complicated. However, one cannot know this, until they get there, in their circumstance. Other things are then revealed, such as, one can live happily there, without sexual motive, justification, or expectation.

So I learned, God has means to help us, but what they are, and how He uses them, is none of our business. His timetable, He also keeps to himself. If only we knew how important is faith, and our ability to trust God, we could relieve ourselves of so much frustration, and self reliance. We could settle ourselves in the comfortable, cushioned seat of God's love. One of the ways we all know we are alive is, to consider the body in its magnificence. Aside from the entities of blood, bone, flesh; and sinew, each body is given a Libido, which measures the sexual urge, instinct, or drive. What makes us so fearful of not getting sexually fulfilled is, while the body is healthy, the libido is also healthy.

These two entities do not operate independently of each other, they are intertwined. Each one tells the brain when there is a problem, and the brain decides the outcome. When we know something is wrong, we do not always have answer to the problem. When I was at this place, I utilized my faith, and fell on the mercy of God. He so graciously met me with everything needed for wholeness, and happiness within His providence.

SECTION TWO

HUMAN INFRASTRUCTURES
And
SKILLS FOR QUALITY LIVING

CHAPTER ELEVEN

RELATIONSHIP DYNAMICS

Back to the time of my social cognizance at about age four or five, I began to exercise the gift of independent thinking. I had a keen sense of the importance of relationship development because it connected me, and whomever I was interacting with, in three ways. The first was acceptance, then agreement and last, pleasure.

At such an early age I did not know those elements were basic to the dynamics of developing relationships. However, lingering in my psyche was a knowing, that the feeling was right, and decent. I felt my soul and spirit was intertwining and confirming that we human beings were in proper communication.

Just as the environment and the universe are ordered, so were relationships between people. Our bodies as well as our spirit assist us in our relationships by reporting our honesty by way of reflecting our emotions. Our eyes, our smiles, and our body language affirm that our behavior is appropriate. In retrospect, I believe getting off to that early start in handling relationships properly, also promoted the start to a healthy mind set, as well as a healthy body.

Especially, did those positive factors aid in my accepting, and receiving others. This gave me the ability to extend goodwill, to be trusting, and to feel secure in relationships. Those things were important because at that early age, it was good to learn how to relate, and get along. People are not born in bubbles, and human beings must learn how to relate to each other.

The importance of family surfaces here; I was fortunate that I had a family; that family was my laboratory to hone and began perfecting my relationship skills. I was unaware of my social and personal deficiencies, yet I could sense at that early age; that if there were some undeveloped social skills; they were forgiven when I was nice.

The same principle Solomon used in (proverbs 10:12), when he said, "Love covers a multitude of sins". Home and family was my embryo, and proving ground, for my preparation to go beyond the boundaries of the protected environment that was home. I watched Father and Mother, in their relationship, noting how they were with each other, while trying to understand why they had different dynamic with us children.

Then, the head work; of putting it all together. From observation I learned the two of them were a unit, and we children were a unit. Together we were family with two respective levels, parents, and siblings. We children never discussed how, or why things were the way they were, we accepted their authority as parents unquestioningly.

We realized that out of our relationships came provisions, protection; and identity. By the time we were ready to leave the nest, we did not know when or how, but we were socialized. My journey broadened out like concentric circles as my age, and understanding progressed.

GIVING RELATIONSHIP ABILITY SPIRITUAL CHARACTER

The next level of developing relationships was my experiences at our family church. For me and my siblings, church was the first real social contacts we had outside the family. All of the relationship skills developed at home, I used at church. They were not taught there, one was expected to have them in place upon arriving. As I displayed my skills, I was rewarded with compliments, and praise.

Church Sunday School was the place where I learned bible verses; how to pray and, how to worship. I learned how to give an offering. If I had two pennies, I gave one. I learned how to sit through old time singing, stomp down preaching, testifying church services. I did not know, however, my social relationship skills were being sandwiched with spirituality. Together the two qualities were like peanut butter and jelly. They gave my character creditability. As I turned school age, I was well ready to enter; and receive some layers of intelligence onto all my home training, as well as my spiritual training. All of that grooming made for very good relationship ability and gave a very solid foundation for life relationships.

On the threshold of entering school, I now had teeth in my relationship ability. To go with acceptance, agreement, and pleasure, I wanted my relationships to be morally sound. That satisfied my desire to be responsible to a higher being rather than just pleasing myself.

This early training was ingrained into my psyche and was holding well for the course of life. It is the fuel that drives this writing. Surely it must have some merit for today's times. Technology has developed to a greater degree and social engineering has drastically affected conversation. Minds, hearts, consciences, and mouths wait for relationship to engage as in the old fashioned way.

TAKING RELATIONSHIP ABILITY TO SCHOOL

I started school, and all I learned at home and at church began to work well for me. It was good many other children had some of the same home training that I had. This made for good social relationships. When there were children who were uncivil, it was obvious they had no home training, and probably no church training either.

In those days whenever, a child exhibited bad behavior, it was confronted on the spot, and it usually was immediately corrected. As with society today, there were always those incorrigible persons who could not even be shamed into civility. They were usually the bullies. Relationships were impossible with such persons.

School proved to be the place a person learned about themselves, even before they were ready to know. Being there, separated out the different layers of the personality. I quickly sensed the limits of my toleration levels, and discovered what and how much of anything I could take. I did not know how to identify what personality type I was; I just knew what triggered certain feelings. I did not like the feelings of insecurity, of isolation, and forced toleration. I determined school was responsible for triggering such misery, and in defense unconsciously shut down. Each time I did this, it cost some of my relationship skills. I knew I could not afford to give up those skills, I needed them to survive.

Later, through trial and error, I learned the feelings triggered, were social. It was hard learning that even young children discriminated on the basis of who had, and who did not have an abundance of equal things. Cliques were formed, and exclusions were decided on by such cliques. Unfortunately, being a victim of such exclusion could have been a devastating thing for me. And it was, but only because it promoted self esteem issues which I dealt with by retreating inward. The price of doing so blocked my learning ability, and brought about my intense dislike for school.

There is no pity desired here for that boy of that period. It is universally true that water sinks and settles until it finds bed rock that allows it to stand. I found that all of the negatives which disenfranchised me from one group ingratiated me to those who needed validation just as I did. Like the water, we found each other and bonded, and loved.

Out of my appreciation, I not only loved, but gave them unwavering loyalty. My ministerial calling was kicking in then in an unconscious way. I became a champion of those who were poor, of low self esteem, and pitiful. Over time even the beautiful group sought whatever it was that I had when they had human or social problems; they gave me a respect that was humbling.

This proves a theory that lends sustaining power to those, especially, the young, who struggle with problems of low self esteem. The salvation of these type problems often wait in social relationships. School is still the big social pool where many problems could be solved. If we could just get our schools back to the place where learning, nurture, and caring; replaces being a repository for social ills.

The key for me, although it was a long time ago, was not to allow isolation, rejection, or bullying to crush my spirit. I realized my adversities were what strengthened my resolve. Nowadays, so many family structures are so fragile they do not give children the social tools of relationship ability. Life itself offers its own peculiar healing for almost all of the problems it carries.

Modem society has created a host of ill advised remedies for social problem solving. Most of these remedies create additional problems, especially is this true in these times of new age; electronic technology. Persons sit side by side and converse by electronic gadgets. They do not see into the eyes of each other therefore, that human spirit of 'we are like spirit beings,' is missed. That missing link speaks volumes about, cyber school relationships, and how they disconnect rather than connect.

TAKING RELATIONSHIP ABILITY TO THE MILITARY

After leaving school short of graduation, and carrying all of the baggage of my personality issues, I was still rich in relationship skills. The playing field was now different because of the way the military operated in ways that civilian society does not operate. In the military rules were changed, all things were done by Line and Staff. The whole bag of civilian relationship skills was turned upside down. In civilian life, I had placed very high value on the application of my skills; because they were the oil of getting along through mutual respect. All of that changed the minute the oath of service was spoken.

The military way of relationships was by acknowledging rank, by saluting, and most of all by following orders. There was no trying to be nice business. Masculinity and toughness was conveyed by sharp, loud, gruff presentation of commands. Correspondingly, recruits and soldiers got respect when they responded in like manner. I had to learn how to relate in this expected manner. It was not easy at first because by personality type, I was not loud, gruff, or tough. The need to survive, and to do well in the service, I did learn the new methods of military relationship abilities. However, I did not relinquish the relationship skills I had learned at home, at church, and at school.

Very much of conveying how military relationships operated had all to do with the way a soldier presented himself; in dress, posture, and confidence. If one met muster in these areas, he/she had met the standard of military relationship. Different from civilian life, the relationship was not spoken so much as demonstrated.

There were opportunities to continue to practice good personal relationships between soldiers who were on the same level. This included especially, those living together in close quarters. I enjoyed the challenge of melding these two relationship styles together, and learned how to refine, and use them interchangeably.

My military service tenure went smoothly, and successfully. Early mastery of relationship skills did help me not only to survive the military, but also to do a lot of good while in the service. I learned how to not only take orders; I learned how to give orders. There was nothing in the military code that said one had to be gruff and crude, to be tough and business like. Therefore, I learned how to convey authority in a manner that commanded respect, without robbing one of dignity. The military gave me many leadership tools that I carried over to my professional life.

TAKING RELATIONSHIP ABILITY TO THE WORKPLACE

After the military, many things had changed in a personal way. I was so much stronger across the board socially, and emotionally. Of course college added to that strength. My relationship skills were now very strong. They enabled me to carry the authority delegated to me by virtue of the many positions I held. How important were these abilities; through relationships I was able to get things done by the way I related to those in my charge. This was always changing because of the different levels of relationship skills on which individuals functioned. The challenge of relating in different ways was achievable because of all of my earlier experiences.

Different from the military way of Line and Staff, the civilian work world method of leadership was Staff and Management. In the military rank said it all. In the work world, position said most of it, and money the rest.

I was always careful to mix caring with compassion, while allowing authority to be the glue. I found that if the source of authority could command the respect of subordinates, the relationship would most likely be sealed. So many times the things learned in the military were the solution to many workplace problems. Some golden nuggets of relationships I used were mined from past relationship trials. A few nuggets were; maintaining a cool temper in the heat of an ongoing difficult relationship, expressing appreciation for expected behavior, presenting a magnanimous spirit when provoked to my last nerve. As an authority figure, I kept the ego level low. I was generous in rewarding, and gracious in understanding, while maintaining constant visibility. My employees were able to observe that I reflected accountability to those over me. This helped them to not be resentful of my asking them to be accountable to my management requirements.

The whole chronicle of any person's work history is a long record of relationships. It is always a sad commentary when in retrospect some relationship behavior might have been of better quality. After such recognition, there is the rest of a lifetime to wish relationship behavior could have been of better quality. The other view is, how satisfying, when a backward look brings good reflections, and rewarding memories. What a blessing when the balance of life is peppered with good relationships formed at work; how comforting, and how enduringly precious.

MY PERSONAL NOTES ON THIS CHAPTER

_____

_____

_____

_____

_____

_____

_____

_____

_____

_____

_____

_____

_____

_____

_____

_____

_____

_____

_____

CHAPTER TWELVE

MARRIAGE DYNAMIC AND RELATIONSHIP

In most oaths, creeds, and charges there are built in requirements that the person taking these, have no option but to agree to the terms. To receive the benefits sought, most people will say yes to all term within such contracts where oaths are required. This theory bears out when the divorce rate is reviewed. One of the most common places to find an example is the institution of marriage.

In my own case I wonder if on October 7, 1956, the date of my marriage to Annie, if I really, really accepted the part of the vows that required me to agree to "until death do us part". At that time, fifty-five years ago I loved, and wanted Annie so much, I would have said anything. I know now that my yes came from a real desire to make our marriage work. However, It was the years unfolding, the going into the depth, and root of love. The separating out; fascination from love, by asking, "Will the real love, please stand up"? It was crying and trying; praying and trusting; coming off of emotional highs, and sinking to depressing lows. It has been the loving one another, so intensely fierce, and consistently long, that the Devil got tired, and went to somebody else. It was the evolving, and unfolding, as well as the one day at a time maintaining; and strengthening what had been started. Never was any magic guarantee that came from just saying vows. It was the work of keeping the vows.

What a journey, what a road, what a vista of kaleidoscopic experiences.

The first five years was learning who we were. This required both of us to strip, and strip until; we were down to real persons that neither one of us knew before. Then it was the long road of blending our true selves into persons with mutual determinations to allow tolerance, and respect to be the vehicle for our journey.

An important reality is revealed here: love evolves over time, out of persons honoring the most basic rules of civility and mutual respect. Every day of their lives together, the work of continued building, and repairing must be done. The tools for this work can be none other than their resolve to honor the vows, a willingness to forgive, and a pledge to be tolerant. The glue to hold all of this together often is hot tears. Faith makes a good frame to hold it all until it sets into permanency.

THE CHILD REARING YEARS

Marital maturity did not come too soon, after the second year our first child Sebrina was born. We had a four year hiatus before our second child Andrew came. Two years later Emory Dana came; we had another two year break before our last child Kelly Dianna came. After ten years our childbearing years were over, and we plunged into our child rearing years. It would take eighteen more years to raise all four of our children to adulthood. At the same time we were plowing our careers. We were both professionals with demanding schedules. However, we never allowed the demands of our careers to have preference over the needs of our children.

At home we always ate together, we prayed together, we played games together; and yes, there were times we cried together. We were hectically happy. In between times we traveled extensively in our Holiday Travel Trailer. For five years these travels gave us family pleasure, and gave our children a unique education they could not have gotten otherwise. Between ourselves, we always honored some basic rules.

- I, as Father was to be acknowledged, and respected as head of our household.
- Annie, as Mother was equal partner, and chief nurturer.
- We would not allow our children to divide us on any issue.
- We would be the first line of authority, and support for our children.

These rules worked well for us, and for our children. When they were all grown up and out of the house, we were in our twenty-fifth year of marriage. During all the years our children were at home; we kept alive our personal relationship. By doing this we never became strangers to each other during those child rearing years. The children knew also that we had a marital relationship as well as a parental one. It was easy to pick up, and be marriage partners again after the nest was empty. We balanced this new level of marriage by integrating our work interest with our personal lives. We continued to travel at every opportunity.

RESPECTING INDIVIDUALITY

Year twenty-five, through year thirty-five we were secure enough to give each other the freedom to reach the ceilings of our individual careers. While in these processes we shared everything, and took active interest in what each other was doing. Care was taken to be sure our interest were our own, and we did not allow anyone outside our personal lives any opportunity to divide, or exploit our marriage. This level of commitment served as our security police; however our marriage was operating on a different level of understanding than the preceding decades. We gave each other full trust of individual career decisions. We each had freedom of movement in our respective professions. We each enjoyed a wide range of friends, and co-workers. In spite of these individual freedoms we shared everything, especially what was going on in our work worlds. Our loyalties to those worlds were different than the loyalties we had to each other that had taken decades to develop.

In each of our arenas, our colleagues knew our spouses. They knew of our marital devotion to each other, and they respected what we enjoyed and considered a heaven blest marriage. Annie soared in her career aspirations, and so did I; as we gave ourselves to our careers. However, when the work day was over, and we returned home; we always reaffirmed our love, and reassured our commitment to our marriage.

TIME BRINGS ABOUT CHANGES

The realities of ageing demands changes, and when they happen marriage is not excluded. We were on the thirty fourth year of marriage when health issues forced my retirement. Annie worked two years beyond my retirement date. The adjustment was easy because our marriage was strong. Even so, some of our most challenging years were between our thirty-fifth, and fortieth marital years. By the same token, some of our most enjoyable events also happened within those years. The single most enjoyable event was our four day cross country trip on the Am Track Train line. We left the Deep South Atlanta, traveled to the Mid-West, on across the Great Desert; and up to Northern California. The trip back was equally as enjoyable by way of Nevada, Arizona, New Mexico, Texas, Louisiana; and home to Tennessee.

Annie retired during our forty-sixth year of marriage. It was then we settled into the pattern of retirement living. This we enjoyed, doing the routine things of survival. We visited with our children, and took much pleasure in watching our grandchildren growing up

The year 2006 arrived marking fifty years of marriage. Our children planned a celebration fit for any King, and Queen. It was shared by many friends, and much family. They and we retraced our journey, and paraded our accomplishments. On this fifty-fifth year we are staying the course of life.

MY PERSONAL NOTES ON THIS CHAPTER

_____

_____

_____

_____

_____

_____

_____

_____

_____

_____

_____

_____

_____

_____

_____

_____

_____

_____

_____

_____

CHAPTER THIRTEEN

FAITH THE SUSTAINING POWER OF MY LIFE FORCE

Over these seven decades of course charting I acknowledge; I could not have made the journey had there not been interventions, and infusions of something greater than anything found on earth. That recognition justifies my describing this intangible force as Supernatural and God given. The Bible calls it Faith, and tells me each being is given a portion called a measure, Romans12:3).

Webster calls a measure: the extent, capacity or dimensions of anything. His definition does not allow me to determine how much faith I was given for my journey. I do know that over my years; as I have squeezed my belief system at times of faltering, it has issued 'more' to sustain me, and keep me from fainting, or "dashing my foot against a stone".

Again, it is the word of God which gives me clarity of understanding when I want to know why, just a 'measure' of faith is enough for my journey. In (Matthew 14:13-21) the story is told how our Lord took two fishes, and five loaves, and feed over five thousand people. He had his disciples to bring all the empty baskets they could find. Then the Lord took the loaves and fish, He blessed them, and began to break the food into the baskets as the Disciples brought them to him to fill. As long as they brought them to him, He continued to fill them from the two fish, and five loaves. This breaking, and feeding continued until the five thousand were feed. Even then, there were twelve baskets of food left over.

The Lord could do this because He being the Son of God, He was the repository of faith itself. Two things were accomplished, He feed the hungry thousands, and restored the faith of the Disciples who were going into town to buy food, forgetting; the Lord who was with them was indeed able to provide.

My measure has truly been more than enough, how many times has my basket been filled because of my faith. Early on, I learned to always allow my faith to exceed the encounters of life that would have robbed me, had I not again, extended my basket that was faith.

WHERE DID IT START

The root of all my beginnings goes back to home. After personal cognizance at about age four, I was still too young to know, or understand anything about faith. Somewhere deep in my spirit, I felt there was something that I knew, that was not like a hand, a foot, or an eye. I could feel its power, its comfort; and it's leading. I also discerned this something came from deep within. It signaled when I needed to cry, it conveyed a good feeling when I did what was right, and a negative feeling when I violated a moral principle. That was my first realization that I was three dimensional; mind, which allowed me to think it through; body, that allowed me to know my flesh reality; and Spirit, which allowed me to feel my intangible, powerful life force.

The Spiritual dimension allowed me to believe that I could hope for something, with a knowing, that was beyond human intelligence. At the time, I did not know this was my belief system falling into place. Therein, was the crucible of my young faith, here, was my God given 'measure' of faith; raw, powerful, eternal. Jesus said to His disciples," If you have faith, the size of a mustard seed nothing shall be impossible for you", (Matthew 17: 20). As I grew in understanding of the separate entities of mind, body, Spirit; and how they worked together, to integrate my being; the dots were connected for me. I began to exercise my faith, to support it with prayer, and to wait upon the Lord.

By observation I could see Father, and Mother modeling faith, yet not understanding what I was seeing. Mother was definite in her faith, because she voiced a desire to see better days during those Depression years. Father displayed a weaker faith, I concluded this because of his pet statement of belief, "the bottom might fall out, "This was more than an oft repeated phrase; it became a pattern that shaped his belief system.

Both parents were in spite of their different degrees of faith, God fearing people. They knew many times faith was all they had to get them from one level to the next. Their faith modeling set the example for me. My teachings, and experiences at our church refined for me, how to couple faith with prayer. I learned both were tethered to God's mercies.

INTEGRATING FAITH INTO LIFE

Growing up, and venturing beyond home brought new revelations. The main one was realizing there were so many dimensions of life. They demanded so many responses that had nothing to do with faith, or God. I could feel the pull of secular, social based pressures. I could also feel the reminders from within, telling me to be true to my spiritual understandings. It became my task to find my way in life while remaining true to my spiritual understandings. Somehow I knew if I did, God would honor my faith commitment. At that very early time keeping faith became a natural part of my life.

As social relationships developed and evolved, it became obvious that not everyone had the same belief system I had chosen for myself. I discovered individuals had all sorts of beliefs. Some of the persons I chose as friends were different in their orientations. My faith was serving me very well, and I enjoyed that extra approbation of Spirit that came from my faith in God.

Each new day part of starting out was to first make sure my spirit, mind, and body were on the same page. Next was to be sure my connection with God was secure. I was then ready to move into the fray of life in the knowledge that faith was my anchor for the day ahead. This approach became ritual for my life, and ultimately became who I am, a person of deep faith.

FAITH AND CAREER

By the time I entered into my career my faith commitment had been in place for many years. Mine was a mature faith that had withstood many storms of life. This faith was not mine to enjoy with just myself and God, it was mine to share with those of lesser faith, especially those in my employ. It was humbling to model my faith for those who were looking for courage, or who were seeking a foothold on some slippery slope of life. In my career

I encountered many persons in these circumstances. Advantage of position provided me many opportunities to help out, of an abundance of faith.

The secular demands of career and leadership sometimes presented conflicting, and tempting choices. These choices often were the difference between career advancement or position stagnation. Other times, they were the difference between salary increases, or receiving the favor of a superior. Some decisions were required for the political expediency of a superior. Too often, individuals holding high positions were on power trips. Such conditions were realities in the work place. Everyday people sold their very souls for positions, money, and power. For persons keeping faith, here were the conflicts, and the temptations. My resolve to be true to my faith was uncompromising; even so, the resolve did not make it easy. It did establish my reputation, and gave me lasting respect.

PERSONAL FAITH

Personal faith is the faith that a person lives in the heart. It transcends one's uprising, down sitting, going in and coming out. It is the faith that confirms; when the mid night hour is lingering, when the knees are bent in prayer, when spirit, mind, and body are in agreement; that God is the ruler of them all. It is the faith that remains when one is alone. It is the faith that sustains when earthly resources are exhausted. Personal faith is the Sentinel keeping watch, it is the Lighthouse ever searching, and it is the Gyroscope keeping the heart upright, when life is topsy-turvy.

MY PERSONAL NOTES ON THIS CHAPTER

CHAPTER FOURTEEN

FRUIT FOR MY JOURNEY

Indeed we do make the choices that decide what life paths we will travel; we choose what shall be the signatures of our lives. We choose what shall be our occupations, vocations; and what practices we will revisit. We choose what life arenas we will play in, and what stages we shall act upon. Starting out on the journey we gather the type of people who will be in our life entourage. During the early unfolding of our lives much of this choosing falls into place rather automatically. The process of it all decides our personas, and shapes our psyches.

It is a good thing that even after we are far down the road of life, we have the option to make changes. Sometimes it is necessary when paths taken earlier, run into dead ends. The reasons we have the Divine privilege of decision making is because God so much wants us to make the decisions that reflect our choices for His leading. When we wisely choose him, He provides provisions for our journeys.

In the mysterious workings of God's ways, He preordains some persons for special paths, and special work. If these preordained persons are obedient, there are not as many opportunities for personal secular choices. They are allowed if a person desires to ignore a calling, and make a conscious decision to lean to their own understanding. Thankfully, I was not too far into my own life decisions before I knew there was a God sent call upon my life. I decided early on to "make my calling, and election sure,"(2 Peter 1:10).

Out of the abundant provisions God provided for my journey it is the fruit that has been so sweetly sustaining. The Apostle Paul aptly describes it as THE FRUIT OF THE SPIRIT, (Galatians 5:22).

THE FRUIT OF LOVE

Love in the secular vernacular has so many multifaceted meanings. In the sense that the apostle Paul wrote, he captured the essence of what pure love was intended to be in First Corinthians chapter thirteen. He was describing that agape love in all of its power, comes directly from God. He makes it clear that while love is definitely in the world, it happens first somewhere deep inside the inner man. Metaphorically, I like to think of its operation in myself as somewhere in the unreachable confines of my spiritual 'situation room'. There the joint chiefs hold their chairs of power; the chair of good, the chair of evil, and the chair of love. Love is the chairman, because it is the only one given the authority to "cover a multitude of sins". In that thirteenth Chapter of First Corinthians verse eight, Paul said, "Love never faileth".

Choosing over all of the forces vying to rule my spirit, I chose Love to rule, to be my lawyer on permanent retainer. Love is the serotonin of my spirit, it is the elixir of my laughter, it is the glue of my compassion; and the food of my faith. It is shipped right out of heaven through the great pipeline of God's unsearchable supply. It is good fruit, strengthening, refreshing, comforting, and sweet.

My Prayer of Thanksgiving for the Fruit of Love

Precious Father, giver of all good things, when I consider how you have loved me with everlasting love, I am thankful.

When I consider how you loved me, when I was substance, in my mother's womb, I am thankful.

When I consider how love was given me, before I could choose it, I am thankful.

When I consider loves faithful recurrence each day, and loving visitation all night, I am thankful.

When I consider loves filling, and sustaining power, I am thankful. Amen.

THE FRUIT OF JOY

When all of the Fruit of the Spirit is ripe, and good, and their juices intertwine; we experience the optimal will of God, giving approbation to our life choices. The savor, the effervescence, the residue of it all, is Joy. It wells up in the heart and overflows into our spirit and gives us holy satisfaction. What a blessing Joy is, it so necessary to the power needed to make our way through the world. This is because the negatives of shame, guilt, apathy, grief, fear, disease, anger; and pride have so heavily invested in the world. These depressing entities seem to fill every shelf of life's market place, while people run over each other to fill their shopping baskets of desire.

Joy opens the emotions to all the delights of holy happiness, and replaces the temporary fix of stuff, and things. My joy has made life much more bearable. Out of its abundance, it is contagious, and continuously blesses others.

My Prayer of Thanksgiving for the Fruit of Joy

Oh God of glory; the author of joy. Thou, who witnessed perfect joy at the creation of the Heavens and the Worlds,

Thou who knew mankind would need something, to fill and satisfy his spirit; you made possible holy joy.

Thank you Father for my joy, that comes from your inexhaustible supply of love. Amen

THE FRUIT OF PEACE

There is nothing like unto the peace of God. The Apostle Paul said, "it passeth all understanding." God not only designed it to be in the world, He laid it upon Jesus to offer it to mankind on an individual basis. It is free, and our world is so much in need of its blessings. I knew very early that I needed it, and wanted it, to calm, bless, and sanctify my spirit.

Over the rocky roads of time, in and out of events, and circumstances, Peace, has been my salvation. Through all of these turbulent decades it has given me resignation, and confirmation of who I am, and whose I am. I especially need it for the place I am, and times I now face.

God in His wisdom has provided in such a way that if one has it, they can share it with others who will receive its blessing. This Peace is powerful, contagious, and inexhaustible.

My Prayer of Thanksgiving for the Fruit of Peace

Precious Father; Oh thou, the reservoir of Peace,

Thank you for Jesus, who through His sacrifice, has made peace possible in the world.

Thank you Father, that He has made the same Peace possible in the hearts of believers.

Thanks you Father for making this Peace possible in me. Make me an instrument of thy Peace. Amen

THE FRUIT OF LONGSUFFERING

So long a time has our Father God sought to reconcile us unto himself. So long a time has his centerpiece, the joy of all His creation; humankind, rebelled against his love. Generation after generation since Adam, have perished because of disobedience, and rejection of restoration. Yet this mighty, precious grace and mercy of God continues to offer redemption. Looking in the worlds' corners there is cursed evidence of man's failures, and pitiful attempts to fix it by his means. Nothing of human strength or wisdom seems to work.

Looking through this dismal cloud of human failures, we can see, and understand and testify that God indeed is Longsuffering. Especially, for believers there is redemptive recognition, I do accept God's longsuffering because I live by the mercy it extends me.

The fruit of longsuffering is not to nourish only elect peoples, or religions; is for all who will receive its forgiveness, and healing properties. This fruit is a gift from God.

My Prayer of Thanksgiving for the Fruit of Longsuffering

Oh loving God, how I thank you for your unconditional love. For loving me while I learned how to love.

For loving me while I strutted on the stages of ignorance, pride, and self sufficiency

For extending the gift of longsuffering to me, thank you for mercy, and for grace. Amen.

THE FRUIT OF GENTLENESS

After I and my siblings were full grown we were jointly working on a tribute scrapbook for one of our Mothers birthdays. It featured all ten of her children. My sister Carolyn was spear heading the project. She asked each of us to provide a photograph of ourselves that Mother would like. Carolyn arranged the pictures in the book, in birth order, and artistically placed them in the book.

She then asked Mother to make a list her children, and put under each one's name one word to describe them. Mother placed under each siblings name the adjective that best described their person. The adjective Mother placed under my name was gentle. When I realized how she saw me, I was very humbled. Since that time years ago, I have tried to live up to my Mother's opinion of the kind of disposition she determined I possessed.

To paraphrase Webster, he said this person would be given to be gentle, soft-spoken. They would be kind, and even-tempered, cultured, and refined in character and conduct. (2 Timothy 2:24-26), corroborates Webster. To encounter such persons in today's world is pure delight, and enjoyable relationship.

My Prayer of Thanksgiving for the Fruit of Gentleness

Dear Lord, how gracious are you my creator, to bless my spirit at the time of my birth, by giving me the attribute of gentleness?

So wonderful is this attribute that even in its quietness of approach, it is powerful in its quality to deliver peace, and comfort.

Thank you Father, for fixing such a spirit in my persona, and please oh Lord, bless and give permanence to this precious gift. Amen

THE FRUIT OF GOODNESS

Greek scholars set the bar for achieving goodness so high it was daunting to even think of reaching such a state. When one considers the evil forces in the world, goodness is very much needed. According to the word of God, goodness is achievable because it does not come from the world; true goodness comes from God. Its capacity is built into man's soul and spirit. It is activated, and regulated according to man's desire to serve, and please God. When such desires are embraced, man's life, and conduct becomes God-driven.

It is then the state of goodness pervades the spirit of man, and his very living becomes virtuous, kind, and benevolent. He then transcends the state of being good, he is transformed into good.

One could conclude as the old saying goes, we are looking for goodness in all the wrong places. We look for it in the world, when in reality our adversary Satan; manipulates the things, and stuff of the world. Goodness is appropriated to the heart of man from God. It has the capacity to fill the earth if man would be the transport. We need more transporters; God does not run out of goodness.

My prayer of Thanksgiving for the Fruit of Goodness

Benevolent God, I know your plan for me is to be a recipient of your goodness, help me to be obedient to that plan.

Mold me, fix me, make me, fill me; that I may be a fit vessel of transport to take your goodness everywhere in the world.

Grant Father, the time when all the earth will experience the full power of your goodness. Amen

THE FRUIT OF FAITH

I cannot use the word magic to describe this fruit, yet its properties are so powerful, it is indescribable by human standards. Magic suggest there is some trickery, or occult influence. Since faith comes from God, I know there is nothing magic about it, it is real; it is Supernatural.

Theoretically, faith has the capacity to get underneath the belief system, and pry it loose from rusty doubt. Then faith, in its supernatural power, inflates the belief system to the point it can sustain, any latent reality.

While faith sustains the latent reality, it or they, marinade in God's will, until He releases the fulfillment of the reality. Then faith has done its work, and remains.

I use these practical ways of understanding faith, and all of the Fruit, so I enjoy the full essence and strength; and my spirit id nurtured.

My Prayer of Thanksgiving for the Fruit of Faith

Faithful Father, my spirit is overwhelmed by your mighty power, especially the power of faith.

It allows me to move confidently in the world, and to believe all things are possible.

Thank you for your faithfulness throughout all ages, and faith to know you will be there in the ages to come.

Thank you for the peculiar manner in which you have made me, it is so awesome.

Thank you for knowing I exist in this vast universe. Amen

THE FRUIT OF MEEKNESS

Growing up, and before I had developed an ego system, my spirit had a penchant toward meekness. My meekness was not so much of a submissive nature as it was of a disposition to be gentle, and indulgent. I quickly learned that society did not have much respect for meekness; it was too often interpreted to be weakness. Somehow I had a knowing that there were stronger connotations for meekness than commonly entertained. This encouraged me to take the risk of not denying the overlay of my personality that identified me to be of meek disposition.

As my life progressed I noted in every arena of my relationships; people too often mistook my meek spirit as a signal that unwarranted liberties could be taken. This was not upsetting to me; I just did not allow their misjudged intentions to go forward. Neither did I feel it necessary to upbraid persons when they misjudged. My meekness was my strength, and after people learned the kind of person I was, they were able to enjoy the fruit I shared. It was the fruit of Meekness.

Throughout my life, and storied careers, I used this gift of meekness to bless others, and accomplish many task which otherwise might have been quite difficult to achieve.

My Prayer of Thanksgiving for the Fruit of Meekness

Dear Lord, Thou who has searched me and known me, and given me a unique spirit, that of meekness.

Thank you for developing my spirit, and for appointing me to use it to thy glory, and service.

Thank you precious Father, for molding me

FRUIT OF SELF CONTROL

Self control and temperance are used interchangeably in the scriptures depending on the translation. From a Spiritual point of view it has all to do with the control of one's appetite, and passions. I was fortunate in that being raised in a very austere environment, there was no temptation to splurge on anything. Father and Mother insisted there be no acting out, or drama in behavior. Given these circumstances temperance/ self control was a natural part of my development in the home.

My spiritual training stressed self control just as my home training had done. There was no wiggle room to get around not being well grounded in self control. This fruit has served me well while staying the course of life. The great benefit of self control is the opportunity to model for others, and allow them to observe the order it brings to relationships, and life.

My Prayer of Thanksgiving for the Fruit of Self Control

Thank you Precious Father, for giving me the fruit of self control that I may give all of myself to your service.

Thank you Father, that my mind, spirit, and body are governed by your will.

Thank you Father, that my spirit joins with your Spirit and allows me to be one with you.

MY PERSONAL NOTES ON THIS CHAPTER

CHAPTER FIFTEEN

SPECIAL MEMORIES FROM ALONG MY JOURNEY

We have come a long way since the opening pages of this book. I cannot close it without sharing some of my most tender memories, and stories. They come from various periods of my life and travels. The flavor of the memory will tell you the period to which it belongs.

MOMMA MAY WE GO OUT AND PLAY

Bright sunlight illuminated the morning sky gushing it's brightness at the highest point of the roof. It painted the wall just under the eaves as it began its downward crawl, slowly covering each siding board. The liquid gold flowed, melting the dew, dissolving the shade, splashing transparent gold; causing the boards to emit steam. Early quietness ... gentle power ... heaven unfolding golden glory of the morning. Me, watching in astonished wonder; as God went about His work.

BETWEEN THE HOUSES

We siblings played between our house and the house next door. We cared less about the world beyond our yard. That precious space marked our boundaries; to us it was the greatest space on earth.

Our imaginations were very fertile, from them came the games we played, and the makeshift toys we made. There our park; there our playground, and all our imaginary lands. There were all our childhood fancies, acted out between the houses.

THE WONDERFUL BACKYARD

The lone peach tree near the outside water spigot lifts its green leaves, helped by the teasing breeze. The sun, and the leaves await their orders from the wind, they are eager to begin their play. When it begins, they shimmer, they glint, they twirl, they lift; and they laugh.

They play their game of spinning to keep me from winning. I see orange, then gold, then green, or was it brown; no, it is in between. All the magic of the centuries, all the tricks of ancient eons, nature's elements remember.

PLAY DAY IS PASSING

By the noon hour the sun has moved down the boards on the north side of the house. It spattered its brightness all over our world; that space between the houses. Now it starts to climb upwards the boards of the house next door, leaving the shade in its wake.

A new ambiance comes in with the afternoon bringing clouds. They interrupt the brightness, changing the tone of the day. The freshness of the morning is over; the bright presence has lessened. The hours mature as earth blends with sky, and eternity is present as the day marches forward. What a blessing to be in the day and exempt from its brief cycle.

THE CLOSING OF THE DAY

I watch the sun settling in the west, as the strong stillness is felt. How unsettling, and beautiful, the setting sun as it as it gathers all its light. Now slowly, darkness tiptoes across the land, stuffing corner, covering the sky; filling every void. Out of the stillness, the last throes of Day scream ... Night! After many decades nature has not lost the wonder it shared with me when I was a child. I hope these sketches of nostalgia last until heavens beauty be their replacement.

ANOTHER STOP ON MY JOURNEY

Near the end of my career in education it was a great privilege to have an assignment requiring me to travel across the beautiful State of Tennessee. All along the way, I saw and experienced much that is noteworthy of sharing.

THE RUTLEDGE FISHERMAN

My day had been long and productive, driving in the late evening traffic made me eager to get to Rutledge. I wanted to get off the road, and get in place for the next day's work. After a restful night I rose with the dawn of the next morning. Getting ready for the day ahead, my mind was boiling, over the tedious details of the work awaiting me. I was anxious about finding the school I was to visit, and what attitude the Principal might be wearing; and what kind of staff was in place. Each new day found me excited about being in a new city, a new school; and with a new staff. I mused at how my job as a state Educational Evaluator was always challenging and exciting. After a good night's sleep, the new day was no different.

Fresh and rested I left my motel room, feeling the chill in the air as I headed to the motor court restaurant. The thick fog from the nearby lake made for a damp cold walk from my room to the ramp of the restaurant entrance. Upon entering, the waitress ushered me to a table across from a gentleman dressed in causal sports attire. He looked up from his menu, and very heartily said, "good morning". Thrilled and surprised, I responded saying, "and a good morning to you sir!"

After placing my order, I heard the smiling gentleman say, "I hope the fish are biting today" as he looked directly at me. Returning his friendliness, I quipped, "oh, are you going fishing?" he answered, "fishing is all that I do." I asked him, "Are you on vacation?" Responding he said, "I am the host of the television show, Tennessee Fisherman", from that point on there was no prompting my new found friend. With his face complimenting his voice, details poured out of him concerning Tennessee lakes, fish, weather conditions, bait: and boats. He gave me instant knowledge of the game fishing industry, and the immensity of fishing in its own right as a sport. Enjoying his expertise, and his charm, I prompted a few questions of my own, and again, I reminded myself of the benefits, and joys of my own work.

Finally, as though remembering he was not alone he asked, "By the way, what is your line of work?" I responded by giving him details of my job and my travels. He was impressed, however, his pride over being a professional fisherman, was overwhelming. Yet, we were both enlightened, as we mused over our similarities; at the same time respecting our vast differences. Before we parted, I asked him "do you know any good fish stories"? Friend said, "a few".

Smiling I teased him about the fellow who loved to tell fish stories, but never finished one. He relished telling them, and they got bigger with the telling. Everyone in his village knew of his fish tales; one day the old man died. As he was approaching the heavenly gates he saw Saint Peter. He thought, he was fisherman, I will ask him a question. He asked, "Saint Peter, does the Lord allow fish stories up here?" Saint Peter said, "Well, sometimes, I think it will be alright for you to tell a few." Happy with the prospect of sharing his fish stories with everyone in heaven, the old man started on through the heavenly gates. Suddenly, Saint Peter called after him, He said, "oh, by the way, Jonah is up here also!" My new friend and I laughed so hard everyone in the restaurant looked our way. As we cleared our throats, we both saw the trailer pulling the boat, and all the accompanying equipment. A television camera crew followed. My friend said "my crew is here now"! I responded, "Have a Good Day."

ANCHORS FOR DEEPER DEPTHS

I knew a man who for many years had lived a totally secular life. He had heard of the existence of God, however, gave no particular attention to wanting to know Him on a personal basis. Literal and professional as he was, he just did not want all of the hassle that is sometimes attached to the practice of religion.

Much later after passing the half century mark he was stricken with a catastrophic disease. Many doctors attempted to stop the physical deterioration to no avail. In desperation, the man turned to God for help, and for healing. He grew close to God in that relationship. He found so much peace that he lamented that he came to Him so late in his life. He also lamented because he now knew the unspeakable joy which overshadowed his burden of suffering, came from God.

Each day it seemed that the man was experiencing even deeper levels of faith. One day his suffering was exceptionally severe. While I was ministering, and praying for him, he blurted out, "is this a good day to die?" My heart fell, and I could hardly answer. Quickly recomposing, my answer was this, the joy of the salvation you feel today is given against a day of more terrible consequences. When that day comes, the joy of your Salvation will be your anchor for those deeper depths.

I n further comforting, I went on to say that when the day of our dying comes, often there is no time to seek inspiration, or earthly help. If help comes, it most likely will be drawn from the reserve vaults of our souls. This is when the promises of God become our reality for that moment. They are given when we step aside from our cares, and walk with Him. To do this, one must be patient enough to allow Him to speak life, forgiveness, and healing into our hearts. Then when troubled waters come into the basement of our lives ... our hearts, and spirit remembers, the very words of the Master, "I will never leave thee, or forsake thee, even to the end of the age". (Heb. 13:5).

TRANSCENDING SUFFERING

I knew all about being a Pastor, and leading congregations. This was a minister's turf. I thought I had been all over this field of that experience. Then a fellow worker fell ill with terminal cancer. We were both Principals in our school system. We did not run in the same circles, but we were civil to each other in a live, and let live kind of way. I was a Minister, and Friend was a Player.

After Friend fell ill it was obvious that he had no track record of spirituality or religious experience. He had no close ties with any minister, or church. He did not have ties with people who claimed to be Christians. After extensive travel, seeking various treatments he came before our group to tell of his plight, and say goodbye, it was a very sad day.

It was not long before Friend took to his bed, it became obvious that he would not get up. Finally, it was announced he had about three months to live. For all the time before, Friend and I knew we held a disdain for each other's life styles. However on the surface we maintained a visible respect for each other. It was then that I understood that even though I did not agree with his lifestyle, I did not offer to share mine. Had he rejected it, I should have offered him the alternative that I knew was better than the choice he had made.

Decency and conscience told me I had to go to him, and offer my service of ministry. I wondered if he would receive me, and my offering. All of my calling, spirit, and training told me I must go. Upon presenting myself, I laid out a plan of ministry for Friend. He listened agreed, and was grateful for my coming. First we prayed seeking God's forgiveness for allowing our human frailties to have kept us apart for so long. Then we pledged ourselves in repentance and forgiveness. Friend expressed a desire to know God intimately before he left this world. We began by giving ourselves to prayer. Painstakingly, he began talking to God. He made a list of persons he wanted to forgive, and ask forgiveness from. I brought these persons to his bed. He confessed, and lamented, all the ways he had rejected God's reconciling.

During that three month period I watched a man become transformed from natural to Spiritual, and embrace intimacy with God. His salvation pilgrimage made me examine my commitment to Christianity. I learned the reality of death of the body, and life of the Spirit, and most of all how to know God in spirit as well as putting the body through motions of morality.

One day Friend, and I were praying. After we finished, the dying man across the hall sent for me. He confessed that he had been afraid to face death however, after observing Friend across the hall, he was now, not afraid to die. He had been listening to our confessions, and prayers. He had been analyzing all of the supplications coming from Friends room.

Friend's time was drawing to an end, the months I had personally ministered to him had galvanized our friendship, and spirituality. Friend, and I, during this short span of time had grown as close to God as anyone could hope. He had learned how to access his suffering to find peace with God. He was preparing for his soul's transition to his heavenly home.

Routinely now, friends and family gathered to keep vigil in the evening hours after work. Hospital staff brought in extra chairs to accommodate the overflow. Friend was a school principal, and it was National Secretary's Week. He wanted to honor his secretary from his hospital bed. In the room was a mix of family, friends; his secretary, and his staff. There was finger food, and deserts. Everyone was enjoying the occasion.

Within that brief gathering, all of those persons came to know each other in ways they did not know was possible. Each person was handling the preciousness of life, displaying their finest selves. They were taking turns, pouring the milk of human kindness, and spreading the oil of emphatic compassion. We all knew the end was near for our mutual friend. As everyone sat in sympathy, and sorrow; Friend suddenly blurted out, "I wish all of you had what I have."A shudder of horror came from the group almost simultaneously.

Later, as Friend and I talked alone, I quarried as to why he had made his earlier shocking statement? He explained, "My life before my affliction was devoid of God, and pretty much obscene. My suffering has brought me face to face with death. It has forced me to profess hope in God. I have come to know God through Jesus Christ His Son. In Him, I have found a peace, a refuge, forgiveness, and the promise of Eternal Life beyond my suffering." "My wish, was that I wanted each of my family, and my friends to experience God's redemptive love, as I have during my illness"

Later in the week, Friend's Life Force was ebbing, as we held hands he began to pray and he said, "If I can't finish, take it up for me." Somewhere, during his praying, he became quiet, he had gone home, talking with the Lord. The impact of the transition that was happening to Friend those last three months of his life; touched many other lives. Many of those lives were other players. I had been in the ministry for twenty-four years before the opportunity of ministry to Friend happened. In all of my Preaching, and Shepherding of Gods flock, that experience spoke more volumes to me than I can record.

- ✓ The gifts of ministry given to those called, is not for their personal benefit. These gifts are to be freely given to those in need.
- ✓ Ministers cannot lead anyone to God without knowing Him intimately themselves.
- ✓ Latent repentance, in the sinner's heart, is often more sincere than the indifference in the heart of some Christians.
- ✓ Godly sorrow works repentance and put us in position to receive redemption.
- ✓ God's mercy prepares the spirits of those who know Him for their heavenly transition.
- ✓ Prayer is the most effective key to unlocking God's mercy.
- ✓ God is an ever present help in time of trouble.
- ✓ God is faith and the etcher of those FINGER GRIPS,
- ✓ even before we need to reach and hold on; or when we have exhausted all of our fleshly and earthly survival strategies.

It is so good when at the intersections of life; knowledge, circumstances, people, places, the physical, and the Spiritual all come together like strangers meeting on a corner. As it was with my sick friend; in his hospital room many diverse strangers were brought together because of their dying friend. While there, they saw God working with their friend, and themselves.

Each person went home with blessings. They each had witnessed Spirit and body honoring God's commands. Each had instantly bonded to the other without examination or qualification. This was because unconsciously each for the sake of a friend had left their ego at the door. Each made a once in a lifetime decision to, for an unspecified amount of time, relate on a Spiritual level rather than a physical level.

How wonderful when people allow the integration of physical and Spiritual to drive relationships. What a leveling agent the Spirit is when we allow Him to remove the ingredient of subjectivity from our hearts, and replace it with humanity.

MY PERSONAL NOTES ON THIS CHAPTER

CHAPTER SIXTEEN

WHITHER CAN I GO FROM THY SPIRIT
(PSALMS 139:7)

My musings and writings have taken me up and down my appointed paths in retrospective review. I have been privileged to even review some side trips I took that I did not plan. I am thankful to acknowledge how God always led me back to the main road that He intended for me. I could not have arrived at these three score and ten plus had He not foreordained for me, that mustard seed, or that measure of faith even before I was born.

Most of the journey has been defined by social and human interactions, mingled with circumstances; and places. I talk a lot about family; people I have worked with, and people I have met. I have mixed in stories of faith about the lives of others. In all of this, again, and again one can sense an unbreakable thread of faith as it ties human lives together.

This thread of faith has helped me to see beyond just a world view. It allowed me to open the window of soul, and see heavenward; and make connection with my maker.

My journey had not just been a body experience it has been a Spiritual journey in an earthly body. So my life in the body has been lived with God and with man. God gave me the privilege to choose His Spirit to have the rule and have authority over my life; rather than me giving authority to the flesh to rule over my spirit.

Every leg of my journey, faith flowed from God's Spirit, and fed my man spirit when it was weak. During my youth, those times when I was spiritually senseless, God kept my measure of faith in latency until I could understand His call on my life.

Overwhelmingly, the Spirit's guiding influence has been a map, and compass for my life. Especially, has He been a force since my full commitment to living a Christian life. That same Spirit watched my substance in my mother's womb, and accompanied me into the world. When it is time to leave, He will be the only entity empowered to accompany me back to God.

THE AGE OLD QUESTION OF DAVID

As a small boy it is storied how David's great gift of music was soothing even to the sheep he kept on the hillsides. His Father Jesse knew he was blessed and highly favored of the Lord. When Samuel saw him he knew David was anointed. God's Spirit was upon him wherever he went, and whatever he did. Later in his life when he acted ungodly, God never withdrew His Spirit from David.

It was late in his life near the end when David reviewed his lifetime goings and comings. He admitted, even when he was disobedient; God's Spirit was there to remind him whose he was. He asks the question and at the same time confirms the answer. There is no place to go where God's Spirit is not there. The depths of the ocean, the bowels of the earth; and he said "if I take the wings of the morning, behold Thou art there" (verse 9).

MY PERSONAL NOTES ON THIS CHAPTER

CHAPTER SEVENTEEN

THE SEASONS OF MY LIFE

As faithful as my years came and went, the seasons of my life came and also passed. Each one bearing a varied mix of fortune, destined to leave its intended impact. While many seasons did not bring what might have been expected, the outcomes always left a beneficial impact, often not recognized immediately. Many times the benefit was not for me, but for someone else through me.

THE SEASON OF WONDER

What a great blessing it is to adopt an attitude of nostalgia and go backwards down memory lane, and recapture that brief period of wonder. A time before the hard veneer of experiences had dulled the view of things in nature. A time when I could see her colors in their brightness, and their richness; when I had the innocence to see the elements intermingling in play. That time, when I could sense the sweetness of people with no fear of anything more, or less. It was a time of pre-world exposure when the cocoon of love, and home was warm and safe.

THE SEASON OF DISCOVERY

A summer rain was filling the sidewalk gutter with water that flowed in a constant strong current. Some invisible ancient voice from eons ago, told me to imagine the pop cycle stick was my boat, and the gutter was my ocean. Placing the stick on the water, it took off in the strong little current. I ran after it with the kind of imaginative joy only a boy could experience. I was discovering the inter-workings of my environment. I was seeing all of the things in God's heaven and earth, each entity doing only what it could do, but all, in concert.

THE SEASON OF RESPONSIBILITY

Responsibility is so important to successful living. It makes the natural order of things go smoothly. Charged to be responsible I was off to school with the understanding that if I were to learn, it was my responsibility to study and apply myself. That carried over into other area of life and was cultivated into a lifestyle. Responsibility also taught me to do my share of assigned chores, and to do them well. One of my responsibilities was to check on the elderly on our street. Do anything they requested, and never charge for my service. I learned to be dependable, to be honest, and to be respectful just by being responsible.

THE SEASON OF CONTRIBUTION

My Mother and Father like many other parents must have hated to farm me out at such a young age to work. Times were different and there was no stigma attached to work. I saw many other boys holding jobs to help their families and themselves. I missed a lot of play but I also learned so much, perhaps too much. Our family was in a time of economic desperation, and my contribution helped.

THE SEASON OF SUFFERING

I had a long season of illness, and suffering, and learned there is a season for such. I know this because God sustained me through it all. In His great mercy He granted healing, and restoration. What I really learned during that season was that God did not need my permission to put me in the position of suffering. Since I claimed to be His, He did not need my permission to use me in His plans. In gracious thanksgiving, I can see how He achieved His will through my suffering.

THE SEASON OF BLESSING

All up and down the roads of my journey I see the evidence of blessings. Each season has given me more than I have needed. There have been so many until those who are near and dear have benefited from the overflow. These blessings for the most part have not been sought they have flowed freely out of Gods goodness and great mercy.

Every day they have been counted, and shared. The strange thing about blessings is they are hidden in what we sometimes call misfortune. Other times they are hidden in illnesses, and many times buried in unfortunate circumstances. The important thing is when they are found, they are of no value unless they are given away in love, and generosity.

As my journey unfolded and blessings came so profusely I learned how to invest in them in order to get a greater return on their offerings. By doing so, there was that much more to share. Blessings are teachers also. They taught me many times, that God is always on time, and He is always faithful.

MY PERSONAL NOTES ON THIS CHAPTER

_____

_____

_____

_____

_____

_____

_____

_____

_____

_____

_____

_____

_____

_____

_____

_____

_____

_____

CHAPTER EIGHTEEN

THE CLOUDY DAYS OF LIFE BROKENNESS

This condition is so common to our world and our times. Media has brought the world together in such a way that we know everything almost instantly, and we can glaringly see into every corner of the earth. In spite of this miraculous progress, there is hardly a place or a spot on the planet devoid of brokenness.

Is there a remedy, a cure or a respite from its misery? May we not forget that fateful day that Jesus situated Himself on the Mound of Olives, and brought the good news of deliverance to all who would hear, especially, was he speaking to those who were suffering from the devastation brokenness inflicts.

The Bible, in (Matthew 5:5-10) tells us that Jesus looked out upon the people with compassion. It was then, He began to speak to them, and as He spoke He changed their brokenness to blessing. He did not call the names of individuals; He called the name of their brokenness. Jesus is still a heavenly, potent advocate for anyone needing a blessing, for whatever kind brokenness attacks those who follow Him. Our world certainly needs all the help it can get, especially supernatural help.

The world has gotten so much bigger since Jesus brought that message of hope. There are so many who follow other persuasions of religion. There are longstanding feuds yet unsettled, dating from the days of Isaac and Ishmael. Wars rage as nations and men fight for power and land.

After two thousand years, no message has replaced or given more hope than Jesus' message. Good men will need to continue to carry it and offer it through good works. Powerful, spiritual living can bring into reality Jesus' prophetic prediction, "ye shall do greater works" (John 14:12).

HURTING

Hurting is the antithesis of being comforted, therefore I am not overwhelmed at its threat. It is a multi-dimensional nemesis with tentacles that reach down into the soul. Its pain is what is felt that we describe as hurting. This hurting is a powerful agent of misery that can go beyond the primary recipient and allow its residue to contaminate loved ones. It is so devastating, and pervasive that the whole world can feel its impact at the same time.

In spite of the heinous aspects of hurting it also is beneficial to the human spirit. It is an irritant like unto a tear in the eye when it washes out foreign objects. It is the oil of the conscience when it needs to be. It is an alarm, when we are not aware of encroaching diseases. It is an advertiser of the soul's tenderness. Hurting is a persecutor and purifier.

Hurting can be a blessing when friends or loved ones are in trouble, or in need of resources or comfort. The kind of compassion that issues forth from a person who has been tempered in the fires of suffering is precious and healing. Hurting sometimes is the only thing other than the Holy Spirit that can drive a penitent soul to prayer.

Now, when examining the dimensions of hurting, it can be done with the understanding; that hurting has its place within the context of why, or what. Then the appropriate treatment can be sought. Two of the best medicines I know for hurting, are Forgiveness and Grace.

LOSS

In discussing loss it first must be qualified as to what kind of loss is being considered. In this discussion I am going to talk about loss from the sense of general loss. Usually, when humans lose anything, we count it as sorrowful. Loss just as Hurt is multi-dimensional.

If any human being these days has trouble defining loss; just look around. Turn on the television, go to the hospital, visit a nursing home, or take a simple walk. Everywhere there is loss, catastrophic loss, tragic loss, personal loss, and corporate loss.

This earth is our home, and like us it is finite, should we expect that there should be no loss? If slipped into such a belief, we are being reminded of the contrary:

Massive Earth Quakes
Vast Forest Fires
Devastating Tsunamis
Destructive tornadoes
Erupting Volcanoes

The list could go on, and on, but enough; we get the drift.

Beyond all of these mentioned catastrophes it seems personal loss impacts the individual more intensely. It is forgivable that persons cannot relate to massive tragedies unless there is some tie that is personal. However, there is always room for sympathy, and empathy. Especially, should compassion be an accessory to humanity. It is a given, if one lives long enough, some tragedy will come eventually come. Sometimes they come and leave, taking their impact with them as they go. Sometimes they come and they linger, and when they leave; they leave a distinct stigma. Other times tragedy comes like a black cloud, it pours misery, pain; and sorrow. It hangs, threatens, billows; and refuses to dissipate.

I n detail I have described Loss and how it could destroy the possibility of hope in those who are weak, or suffering. I mentioned that comfort was the antitheses of Hurting. It is good to know that all of life's misfortunes have deep roots, however the roots of Love. Goodness, Grace, and Healing are deeper, and stronger. These all flow from God's mercy through Jesus Christ.

COMFORT

The word itself is comforting in the light of all the other words that issue negativity. The maladies of earth seem so plentiful it is encouraging to know there are wells of comfort that never run dry. Comfort is not one of those tangible qualities it cannot be seen in abundance everywhere. I t is a heavenly commodity that has to be accessed by pouring the milk of human kindness.

FAMILY

How wonderful when in distress, and there is nowhere to turn. It could be when money is exhausted, trouble is pursuing, or life is ebbing. What a privilege to have a family to give comfort even if that is all they have to give.

Unfortunately there are many persons without family. So many families have been born out of love, and kindness. Those two attributes bond persons so close together, they describe themselves as family.

FRIENDS

A classic illustration of what friendship should be is the ancient story of Job. It depicts a time when he was suffering and in great grief. The bible reports he was visited by his three friends, Eliphaz, Bildad, and Zophar. They came with the understanding that they were indeed friends. After finding Job in a despicable condition they withheld the friendship they came to offer.

They just sat watching him for eight nights and eight days. They did not speak a word. Sadly they decided their friend had committed some sin, and was being punished by God, (Job 2:11).

When persons are ill, or find themselves in trouble, friendship is welcomed, and needed. The sadness in the case of Job was seeing his friends deny him the very commodity they came to offer.

The milk of human kindness is the very glue of friendship. To judge or condemn is the last thing a troubled friend needs, especially when grieving, or in need. In our day, and time we never should fear the desertion of friends in times of trouble. A certainty we know is that friends will fail, however a sure promise is that Jesus never fails. He is a friend who sticks closer than a brother.

Job in his sufferings, and experiencing the denial of his friends; was reminded from somewhere deep within his spirit; that Jesus was in the plan of God's redemption. God opened Job's mouth and spoke into his own ears, and the ears of his friends; the words he spoke were, "I know My Redeemer Lives" (Job 19:25). Job stated that truth long before the reality of that prophecy was fulfilled. We know too, from somewhere in our spirits that "God is a very present help in time of trouble (Psalms 46:1). (Proverbs 18:24 reminds us all, "there is a friend that sticks closer than a brother," His name is Jesus.

True friends are not seasonal

True Friends are compassionate

True Friends are not judgmental

True Friends do not shun truth

True Friends can bear the truth

True Friends are loyal

True Friends Stay the Course

MY PERSONAL NOTES ON THIS CHAPTER

CHAPTER NINETEEN

LATE LIFE TRAVEL

It is strange to awake each morning and find myself at a place in life that is different from any other place I have been before. It always evokes thanksgiving in my spirit, and prompts me to say out loud, "God is good." In youth everything was so automatic, and I was so sure of the way, and the outcome of the day. When I think of all of those years and all of those roads, even the boldness that took me over their paths, I am amazed.

"David said, "night unto night showeth speech, and day unto day showeth knowledge" (Psalms 19:2). The truth of his statement is so potent, how could I not know; I have not come this far alone. So, my cup runneth over with thanksgiving, I know goodness and mercy has not only followed me, but has often gone before.

Just to remember the elasticity of the body, how it literally bounced at the thought of moving. There was the quickness of the mind in thinking and recalling, and that blithe spirit of adventure. Youth challenged me to literally run down my appointed road, and I did. Life was on automatic and moving. Sometimes the moment seemed as though it would last forever even though the pace was swiftly flowing down the streams of time.

The years were interspersed with a mix of good and bad fortune, as youth did its job of providing resiliency. Youth in its spirit and its gifts, has a tendency to mask the seriousness of approaching dangers. We must be responsible enough to be sensitive to the needs of our bodies, and our spirit. When we are responsible during our youth travel; we will not run headlong onto any unsafe roads of youth. The signs are clear, and posted along life's highway.

CHANGE

When youth runs its course, the landscape of life begins to change. Some scenes remain familiar while others take on strangeness. If not careful one might just run on a while before realizing the change has happened. It is a sad commentary when one awakes one morning, and the mind tells the body to move, and it answers, "I just cannot". We know something has happened when we jump up, and we have no buoyancy. How crazy to be thinking, and not remember what we are thinking about. There are many other changes, however my purpose is not to depress as much as to inform. Be ready, and prepare, refuse to be dreadful, because life continues to deliver us to our natural destinies.

TRANSITION

Outside of the physical realm youth moves aside to allow other changes to assume their natural order and place. Children have grown up, and moved on with their lives. The empty nest sometimes prompts tears as old memories creep into the empty spaces of the mind. Retirement also brings its adjustments to the old familiar. Instead of going to work, we go to the doctors. Much time is spent looking for the wallet, the glasses, dentures or the jewelry. Sitting, waiting, and wondering, spending much time in prayer. Days are spent learning how to access ease and comfort out of late life travel. We also wonder how the transition will go when the journey comes to an end.

There are no exemptions when it comes to entering this phase of life. Everyone knows this up front, yet some people travel as thought the road has no end. Too many enter the road of late life travel fearfully. To do this is not necessary because Godly safeguards have been built in every mile of the way. I like to think of them as investments. When honored they pay huge dividends that can be spent only, to be redeemed on the road of late life travel. It is sad to encounter those who took out traveling mercies on youth's road, and did not invest for later travel.

EARLY INVESTMENT FOR LATER TRAVEL

God started all of our earlier accounts, and allowed us to take them in our care at the age of responsibility. At the time we began to travel responsibly, that is when the investing on our behalf should have begun. I have mentioned some of these metaphorical investments in earlier chapters, and in other discussions. Just to refresh, I cite Grace, Mercy, Peace, Joy, Forgiveness, and above all, the investment of Love. Just a minimal investments of any of these made during youth travel, are guaranteed to yield big dividends. God designed these products to yield their dividends especially during late life travel.

Our little personal investments pay us small dividends that we can spend at life's shopping places along our journeys. Those investments are; exercise, health foods, medications, vitamins, and doctors. Such investments only benefit the body.

GRACE

Grace is such a powerful, wonderful word. I can hardly mention it without thinking of it in its Spiritual context. It represents the substitutive work Christ did for all at Calvary. The goodness of it is that this holy work cost us nothing. The grace of God works in other ways such as benefiting the Lords people on their earthly journeys.

When one's faith is properly entrusted to God through Jesus the Christ; grace is sprinkled on the path He knows we all must travel late life's road if we are blessed to live. It reinforces our enhanced spirits which supports our waning bodies. It rebuffs the fear that becomes pervasive in our old age. Again, David said, (Psalms 71:9) do not cast me off in the time of old age; do not forsake me when my strength fails"

That alone on the part of grace will get one far up the road of later life travel. Grace alone softens so many things that were hardened way back on the bumpy road of youth. It not only softens, but it has the ingredients to make even 'old stuff' melt away. Especially does grace wake up the body during late life travel; when it would prefer to sleep away. Grace forgives us when our faces cannot hide our decay, and friends refuse to look away.

Grace is one of the largest umbrellas God uses. It covers so much of the ground His people stand and walk on. I cannot describe its parameters because I do not believe God has any that are discernable to our finite sight.

MERCY

Mercy is easy to relate too, and to be thankful for its benefits. It is the word closest to grace. Many say the two words are cousins. When they work in tandem, what awesome results are wrought? The best way to describe mercy is to review the case of one who has been shown mercy. For me there in no greater example than that mercy granted to one of the two thieves on the cross. That story took place during the time of the crucifixion of Christ. At the last minutes before Christ gave up His life, the doomed thief acknowledged Jesus as the Christ, and asked Him for Salvation. (Luke 23:43), "And Jesus said to him, "assuredly, I say to you, today you will be with me in paradise."

The mercy Jesus granted the thief, translates to every believer's redemption and assurance of Eternal Life. The quality of mercy we give, and receive from each other is only as good as our hearts are pure. When it is given out of a pure, compassionate heart; God honors the grantee, and the grantor.

The abundance of mercy is incalculable. I do not believe it could ever be used up. I wonder if the human race even comes close to tapping into an amount that pleases God. In my life I have been shown so much mercy that I am obligated me to give it abundantly and freely at every opportunity. (Luke 12:48)"For everyone whom much is given, from him much will be required."

MERCY'S WORK

Mercy reflects the quality of the Love of God.

Mercy is God's gift too mankind through Jesus Christ.

Mercy is a heavenly tool, God allows us to use on earth.

Mercy is the currency of forgiveness.

Mercy is sweet spread for sour bread.

Mercy is another chance; undeserved!

MOURNING

"Blessed are those who mourn, they shall be comforted" (Matthew 5:4)

Mourning is the universal expression of grief due to loss of a loved one, or friend. It also happens beyond loved ones and friends. Humankind is so fashioned by God that the contagiousness of the human spirit has a way of gravitating from one human to another. This mysterious bonding is like unto magnets flying to embrace each other when there are no obstructions between. This happens when people allow their spirits to remain free of intentional prejudice. When such prejudice is allowed, it can block the natural processes of bonding. If the bonding process is blocked, the effect is like unto two batteries meeting both having negative ends; they will repel each other. Selective mourning happens when people deny their compassions to others because of differences. Nevertheless mourning is a fact of life. Humans hurt when other humans leave the scene of life.

Mary and Martha hurt so much when their brother Lazarus died, they partly blamed Jesus for his death, (John 11:21). The significant thing is that Jesus loved Lazarus so deeply, He wept when He learned of his death. His Deity did not exempt Him from compassionate mourning.

There is much to learn about mourning from David. When His little son died he refused to eat, or bathe, or sleep. He continued for days in this mode. Finally a grave realization dawned upon him. He realized the child had gone to God who had given him life at first. He arose, bathed, and ordered himself some food. David stated, "He cannot come back to me, but I can go to him."

Living in harmony with each other, and nourishing a love for humankind helps to bear the loss when death comes. Show every kindness to others while they are living. Know what is promised to those who die in the Lord.

Mourning is the hurting of the soul. We comfort the bereaved when we allow our soul to hurt as they hurt, and it flows out in compassionate streams. Mourning is a commodity of our spirit more so than our bodies. That is why the feeling of hopelessness come over us; to remind us that what grieving people need from us, we can get it only form God to give it to them in comfort.

MY PERSONAL NOTES ON THIS CHAPTER

_____

_____

_____

_____

_____

_____

_____

_____

_____

_____

_____

_____

_____

_____

_____

_____

_____

_____

CHAPTER TWENTY

THE INDOMITABLE HUMAN SPIRIT

The human spirit has the capacity to soar to great heights and sink to great lows. These qualities change out on a regular basis depending a lot on the circumstances of the individual. Individuals are impacted by different sets of circumstances. These circumstances in most cases mold, and shape the personality. The personality is a giveaway to the quality of the spirit living within. Whatever the forces, or the circumstances, it is good when the spirit can maintain its indomitability. I have done a lot with the positive forces, and how they impact our lives for good.

There is a lot to be said about the spirits, or forces that promote bad feelings in good people. These are the forces that can warp a personality, or ruin an otherwise positively developing human being. After much consideration and review of how God has dealt with me during some of my hardest trials; I come to this conclusion. There is no value in cataloging the evils or the forces than attack human life and spirit.

These are permitted to rage, kick, scream, destroy and even to kill. They take great joy in pitting lives against each other. They seek to under mind good everywhere it sprouts. They are given to be loud, profane, threatening, and sensational. They do have authority because they are agents of the very repository of all evil. Their authority is regularly reenergized by their leader and guarantor, Satan. The Apostle Peter describes him, (1st Peter 5:8) "Be sober, be vigilant; because your adversary the devil walks about like a roaring lion, seeking whom he may devour".

The unique characteristic of Satan and his forces are they too are spirits. The question is which spirits shall you give sanctuary? Which shall you give entry, which shall you give authority, and ruler ship? Often the frustrations humans   feel come directly from the waging war of Spiritual warfare within. It creates the inability of decision making, and the "I don't know what to do with myself."

These are the times when God vetoes any force or spirit that come against His own. Out of that power and affirmation, the reality of the indomitability of the human spirit comes forth, and holds.

MY PERSONAL NOTES ON THIS CHAPTER

CHAPTER TWENTY ONE

SOURCES OF POWER HOLY SPIRIT

A big key to successful living is knowing, where to get help, or what help is needed. The kind of help I want to particularly discuss is Spiritual help. We tend always to know where to get help for the body, for our appetites; and for our desires. There is great ignorance when it comes to understanding that the spirit life of the body also has needs. It has to be cared for, it has to be nourished; and it has to be cherished.

The body's connection is to the soil from which it came. It automatically seeks and craves what it needs. It will nag, nag, and nag until it gets what it wants. The spirit's connection is to the Father. The spirit is more dependent upon us to want, and desire His presence. That is part of the freedom we have, to receive it, cherish it, or allow some other spirit take its place.

No doubt, that is why Spiritual discipline is necessary, to guarantee the Holy Spirit a place within our hearts. When we do this, we give it the authority to become our life's power source. God supplies His Spirit within us with enough power to oppose any foe; natural, or unnatural; as long as His presence is welcomed.

COME HOLY SPIRIT

Come into this Holy Temple that is set up in the world. Bring the Power God sends, install it in my heart.

Come into this place of flesh, consecrate the space, let thy influence spread outside, make me more than flesh.

Take permission from my soul to be my ruling power, let you authority take control, guide me; orchestrate my life.

Oh holy source of power, flowing from on high, turn on every fleshly switch; let me reflect your light.

HOLY SCRIPTURE

I was thirteen years of age when I accepted Jesus as my Personal Savior. I had been receiving religious training long before my conversion. A major portion of my training was the study of the scriptures. From the beginning the scriptures were instructive and fascinating. They were so compelling I began to studying them on my own. I begin with the Patriarchs, the Prophets, and the Synoptic Gospels. I continued with the Pauline Epistles the First Five Books of Moses; and the general history of the Old Testament. Those were beginnings at a very early age. All of my life I have loved the scriptures as I do at this writing.

All of my life they have blessed me in special ways; on the regular path, and on the side roads. They were a blessing during times of trial, and times of illness. They blessed me when death was doing me like Job's three friends did him. The scriptures are the food that feeds the Holy Spirit; to keep Him strong within our body temples.

A PRAYER FOR THE SCRIPTURES

It was your word that in the beginning created the worlds. It was also your word that became flesh in the person of your Son Jesus Christ, to bring the Good News of salvation to mankind.

Precious Savior, it is your word that guarantees your promise, not to leave us comfortless in this world.

Thank you Father, for your faithfulness and for the power of your word, that keeps us now and throughout eternity.

Thank you Father, for the truth of the word, that goes straight to the heart of every believer.

MY PERSONAL NOTES ON THIS CHAPTER

_____

_____

_____

_____

_____

_____

_____

_____

_____

_____

_____

_____

_____

_____

_____

_____

_____

_____

CHAPTER TWENTY TWO

THE CHRISTIAN CHURCH

Out of the three foundational learning places of my life, the church has been the most influential. I was born into my family through my parents. I reached the age of Spiritual conviction and gave my life to the Lord. That conversion experience is where my commitment and Christian walk began. Fortunately, I was a very young boy just entering my teens. Starting at such a young age was a blessing because it has given me a lifetime of Christian Church experience.

That early beginning has also given me a lifetime certification, and ordination through its auspices. My work in the ministry as a Pastor and Teacher has also been in and through the church. This qualifying gave an operational arena, and launching place to honor my individual calling. I do not wish to give the impression that the church is just a place to find personal fulfillment of career aspirations.

The Church Universal and proper is the fulfillment of God's redemptive plan for mankind. It is the mystery of the ages, which God has revealed through Jesus Christ. Christ being the embodiment of all the Church is intended to be. It is what is symbolized or understood when a person chooses Jesus as his/her personal savior. They are in Christ Jesus and recognize that He is the Head and Body of His Church.

Christ as Head of the Church is given all authority in Heaven and Earth. When one comes to God, he/she come through Christ Jesus. If one will know God, He is known through His Son Jesus the Christ.

MY PERSONAL NOTES ON THIS CHAPTER

EPILOGUE

King Solomon, son of King David, wisely stated, "There is a time for everything under the sun." The fullness of time, and Divine revelation, has confirmed the truth of Solomon's wisdom for me. During my youth, and the years since, Solomon's Ecclesiastes, and David's Psalms, have been the anchors of my spiritual reading. Solomon's third chapter of Ecclesiastes frames the things that time has destined, by putting them in perspective.

Each reading, I was stunned by his wisdom, it literally, jumped off the pages. I committed many of those scriptures to memory. I thought, how beautiful, these words sound, and ring. Then, I realized, no Divine revelations, was sprinkled on their beauty. They were just, wise sayings, the awe I sensed, was poetic.

When I was stricken with cancer, and cure was elusive, I never entertained the thought, that there was a time for suffering." Solomon's wisdom helped me understand, while suffering is not always ordained of God, sometimes it enjoys His permissive will. It is through that will, that God's purposes are achieved. Like many Christians, I unconsciously thought, one of the perks of Christianity was exemption from suffering.

The accumulation of many things, and their consequences brought this erroneous type of thinking to an end. At that pregnant moment in my life, suffering received is cue. Its mighty hand lowered me into the position of affliction. This position, I resented, considering it untimely, and unfair. I did not appreciate how it made me feel. The physical debilitation demanded more than I had to give. Neither did I like the view, the position presented me. It was a view of death. My emotions were full of fear; my eyes were full of tears. My time with God was argumentative, but futile.

I concluded God was angry with me, and further, I was angry with myself. The self anger was because, with this view of death, every sin I consciously remembered was magnified seven times. In retrospect, I was not waiting for God's, judgment, I had condemned myself. This faulty thinking moved me beyond faith. It robbed me of mercy for my suffering, giving way to the disease, to run rampart. Because of my life experience as an individual of faith, I was driven to seek Divine help. Since doctors held, no hope, I knew if I were to have any, it must come from God, through His word.

First, the word's power began to transform my erroneous thinking. I had been allowing my thoughts to be driven by my flesh. By its pain, shame, and whining. Slowly, new understanding came, bringing changes in the things I prayed about. The prayers were no longer about me, but about my desire to know God more intimately, through my afflictions, and suffering. As these changes took root, my spirituality increased, and revelations began to come.

It was then that I knew there is a time for suffering, and also a purpose. My job now was to trust God, and live in His promises. The end result of suffering is not always death, for me it became Life Eternal, instead of life, in the flesh alone.

Now, when I read the scriptures, I am no longer amused, and in awe. With reading, comes Divine revelation. The ring of a passage becomes the voice of God, speaking truth, life, healing, and purpose. It is His words alone that have the power to etch, FINGER GRIPS. It was my faith that allowed me to find them, and hold onto the Solid Rock.